BASKETBALL NOW!

BASKETBALL NOW!

THE STARS AND STORIES OF THE NBA

ADAM ELLIOTT SEGAL

NOW!

SECOND EDITION

FIREFLY BOOKS

A FIREFLY BOOK

Published by Firefly Books Ltd. 2017
Copyright © 2017 Firefly Books Ltd.
Text copyright © 2017 Adam Elliott Segal
Photos copyright as listed on page 159

First printing

Publisher Cataloging-in-Publication Data (U.S.)
Names: Segal, Adam Elliott, author.
Title: Basketball Now! : The Stars and Stories of the NBA / Adam Elliott Segal.
Description: Richmond Hill, Ontario, Canada : Firefly Books, 2017. | Second Edition. | Includes index. | Summary: "Second Edition features 50 profiles of the best players in the NBA today, as well as updated essays on the NBA Draft, the Dunk Contest, the best clutch performances and the playoffs" – Provided by publisher.
Identifiers: ISBN 978-1-77085-925-8 (paperback)
Subjects: LCSH: Basketball players – Biography. | National Basketball Association -- Biography. | BISAC: BIOGRAPHY & AUTOBIOGRAPHY / Sports. | SPORTS & RECREATION / Basketball.
Classification: LCC GV884.A1S443 |DDC 796.3230922– dc23

Library and Archives Canada Cataloguing in Publication
Segal, Adam Elliott, author
     Basketball now! : the stars and stories of the NBA / Adam
Elliott Segal. -- Second edition.

Includes index.
ISBN 978-1-77085-925-8 (softcover)

     1. Basketball players--United States--Biography. 2. National Basketball Association--Biography. 3. Basketball players--United States. 4. Basketball--United States--History. I. Title. II. Title: Stars and stories of the National Basketball Association.

GV884.A1S44 2017   796.323092'273   C2017-904609-8

Published in the United States by
Firefly Books (U.S.) Inc.
P.O. Box 1338, Ellicott Station
Buffalo, New York 14205

Published in Canada by
Firefly Books Ltd.
50 Staples Avenue, Unit 1
Richmond Hill, Ontario L4B 0A7

Cover and interior design: Matt Filion

Printed in Canada

Canada

We acknowledge the financial support of the Government of Canada.

CONTENTS

INTRODUCTION

JUST WHEN YOU thought the NBA couldn't get any better, the 2016–17 season showed up. There was something for everyone this past year. Take Russell Westbrook's historic triple-double season, the first since Oscar Robertson accomplished the feat in 1962. Or James Harden's dominance as he moved to point guard, nearly hitting trip-dub territory himself. There was the usual LeBron James being LeBron James and Steph Curry being Steph Curry. But there was also some very real drama. The Westbrook–Kevin Durant fallout produced two hotly contested games between Golden State and Oklahoma, a city still feeling the sting of Durant's departure. Durant had the last laugh, scorching the NBA Finals en route to his first ring and first finals MVP award. It was a feather in the cap of one of the NBA's best players of the last decade.

It was a breakout season for point guards. John Wall of the Washington Wizards took another step toward stardom, draining a last-second three in Game 6 of their second-round playoff game versus Boston. Kemba Walker in Charlotte, Kyle Lowry in Toronto and Damian Lillard in Portland all took their own steps forward. With the league trending toward three-point shooting over post play, today's NBA is a far cry from that of the '70s and '80s when big men dominated the game. Now the crafty point guard who can drain it from deep is fast becoming the focal point of his team's offense.

And don't forget the young guns and silent assassins who stood out: Andrew Wiggins and Karl-Anthony Towns made slow but steady steps toward establishing a winning culture in Minnesota, and 24-year-old Anthony Davis dropped a 50-point game in October that he bested at the 2017 All Star Game, an effort that earned him All-Star Game MVP honors. And don't forget when sharpshooter Klay Thompson knocked down 60 points in just 29 minutes of floor time in December. Perhaps the biggest breakout star was Milwaukee Bucks forward Giannis Antetokounmpo, who is demolishing the concept of what it means to be an NBA player. Antetokounmpo can play all five positions, and his blazing performance in the first round of the playoffs versus the Toronto Raptors turned heads. He will be one to watch for years to come.

But perhaps the 2016–17 season will be remembered most of all for the MVP race. A strong case could be made for at least five players. It's no perfect science; we all have our biases and favorites. Westbrook, Harden and LeBron were all front-runners for most of the season, but the emergence of several new superstars kept everyone on their toes. Like Isaiah Thomas. How would you like to be the GM in Sacramento or Phoenix watching your former point guard thrive in Boston? Thomas finished top three in scoring and put himself in the middle of the MVP debate. Or Kawhi Leonard, whose dominant performance at both ends of the floor ensured the Spurs didn't miss a beat after Tim Duncan's retirement. In the end, Westbrook came out on top, beating Harden and Leonard for the honor.

It wasn't a perfect season by any means — the Slam Dunk Contest took a step back from the LaVine–Gordon showdown in 2016, and the league was beset with scheduling issues that saw important games sandwiched together and Saturday night marquee affairs in which coaches opted to rest their superstars.

The season finished with a bang, however. Golden State and Cleveland met for the third straight time in the NBA Finals, the first three-peat of the same two franchises in league history. James set the all-time career playoff scoring record, while Durant finally etched his name on the Larry O'Brien trophy. Despite the finals running just five games, the series was fast paced, intense and high scoring (Cleveland dropped 86 in one half!). The rivalry is certain to continue for years to come, and Golden State appears headed toward dynasty territory.

The same questions popped into my head throughout the season: Who's the best player in the league? What's the most intriguing style of play? How is the game changing? And what does the future look like? I don't have the answers. But what I do know is the NBA has never been in better shape. An excellent class of young studs is set to join a group of established veteran stars, creating a healthy mix of old and new. International players continue to arrive in droves, making the NBA a truly global sport. And superstars like Curry, James, Westbrook and Harden continue to push the envelope and defy our expectations.

In this revised edition, we've tried to highlight those stars who have taken the leap to the next level while still honoring the biggest names in the NBA. Some new faces grace these pages as well, notably flashy point guard Isaiah Thomas, Latvian phenom Kristaps Porzingis, small forward Jimmy Butler and rising stars like C.J. McCollum and Karl-Anthony Towns, among others. Although we couldn't include every rising star or game changer, we hope there's something for everyone and that we've been able to capture even a fraction of the record-smashing, jaw-dropping excitement that was 2016–17. Here's to many more seasons like it.

Russell Westbrook, who averaged a triple-double in 2016–17, passes the ball through traffic in a game against the Orlando Magic.

RUSSELL WESTBROOK

POSITION SMALL FORWARD / **SHOOTS** RIGHT / **HEIGHT** 6'8" / **WEIGHT** 240 LB. / **DRAFTED** 2003, DENVER NUGGETS, 3RD OVERALL

CARMELO ANTHONY 7

FOURTEEN YEARS IN the NBA and it feels like Anthony's always been an offensive juggernaut. But the New York native was once a gangly teen at Towson Catholic High School in Maryland and Oak Hill Academy in Virginia before setting his sights on Syracuse University, where he led the Orangemen as a freshman to a national title in 2003.

In one of the deepest drafts in recent NBA history, 'Melo went third overall in 2003 behind the consensus number one LeBron James and the soon-to-be-forgotten Darko Milicic. He made an immediate impact his first season in Denver, taking the 17-65 Nuggets to 43-39, good for eighth in the West. Despite the regular-season success, the Nuggets were ousted in five games by Minnesota, and Anthony would finish second in Rookie of the Year voting to King James. But his strong rookie season — 21 points per game, 6 rebounds and 3 assists — was impressive nonetheless. Anthony would lead the Denver Nuggets to six straight playoff appearances but rarely farther than the first round.

A slow and steady rise up the NBA's career scoring ladder has been a testament to Anthony's talent and willingness to work hard. By his third year, he was averaging 26.5 points per game. He torched the 76ers in that 2005–06 season for 45 points and developed a reputation for hitting clutch game-winning shots. Despite finishing third in the conference, the Nuggets bowed out to the Clippers in the playoffs, and

owing to his most successful season to that point, the Nuggets signed Anthony to a five-year, $80 million deal.

At 6-foot-8 and 240 pounds, he was no longer a gangly teenager who skipped class. He became an All-Star and remained one for four of those five seasons he was signed to the Nuggets, although he finished the fifth season as a New York Knick after a trade partway through 2010–11.

Anthony led the NBA in scoring in 2012–13 on a poor Knicks squad, but what most fans will remember is the colossal 62-point affair at Madison Square Garden on January 24, 2014. He set two records that night: most points by a Knick (previously 60, set in 1984 by Bernard King) and most points ever scored by an individual in MSG (previously held by Kobe Bryant's 61 in 2009). And Anthony didn't even play the

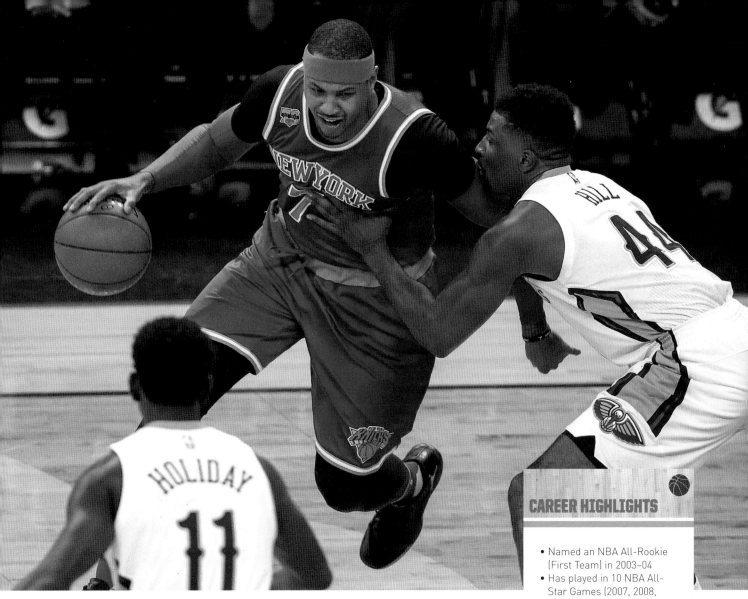

CAREER HIGHLIGHTS

- Named an NBA All-Rookie (First Team) in 2003–04
- Has played in 10 NBA All-Star Games (2007, 2008, 2010–2017)
- Was the NBA scoring champion in 2012–13
- Set a career high in points (62) in 2013–14
- Won an Olympic gold medal with the U.S. men's basketball team in Beijing in 2008, London in 2012 and Rio in 2016

final 7:18 of the game that night versus the Charlotte Hornets. He finished 23 for 25, 6 of 11 from beyond the three-point line and 10 of 10 from the free-throw line, and he even added 13 rebounds, etching his night in the pantheon of greatest performances in basketball history.

"I was just locked in," he said following the contest. "The focus that I had, I felt like it was going to be a good night. There's only a small group of people that knows what that zone feels like." Perhaps even more impressive — he took the second fewest free throws among the 30 60-point games logged since the 1963–64 season.

As Anthony continues his march on the record book, his legend grows — currently he is 25th all-time in points scored, the fourth highest among active players. He's represented his team at the All-Star Game 10 times and thrice won gold at the Olympics.

In 2014–15 he became the 40th player to reach the 20,000-point plateau, the sixth youngest to do so. But all this won't matter in the ring-crazy NBA if Anthony can't take a team deep into the playoffs, something that has eluded him since his days at Syracuse.

The Knicks are still a work in progress on the way to becoming a true contender, and Anthony has committed to staying in his hometown for the foreseeable future. However, the 2016–17 Knicks season, steeped in turmoil, has caused some within and beyond the organization to question whether Anthony will remain a Knick for life. He is still relevant, dropping a 45-point game in a quadruple OT thriller against the Atlanta Hawks. He's still a dependable and valuable piece on any team, averaging 22.4 points, 5.9 rebounds and 34 minutes over the season. But with potential su-

perstar Kristaps Porzingis waiting in the wings, it remains to be seen if the Knicks will continue running a triangle offense through Carmelo, still one of the deadliest shooters in the league.

Will he go down as this generation's Patrick Ewing — the best Knick to never win a title? Or will he be the one to finally deliver New York their first championship since 1973?

POSITION POINT GUARD / **SHOOTS** RIGHT / **HEIGHT** 6'3" / **WEIGHT** 190 LB. / **DRAFTED** 2009, GOLDEN STATE WARRIORS, 7TH OVERALL

STEPHEN CURRY 30

HIS SHOT IS as pure as they come: a sweet stroke that finds nothing but net from whatever corner of the earth he hoists it. Stephen Curry was born to shoot basketballs. Whether it be a full-speed breakout-to-pull-up three or a slash to the hoop, he's graceful and almost effortless. Mostly, Steph Curry is a star.

Born Wardell Stephen Curry II in 1990, the point guard comes from basketball pedigree, the son of former NBA player Dell Curry. Dell spent 16 years in the league and finished his career in Toronto, where his oldest son Steph spent time playing 1-on-1 in shootarounds with Vince Carter and Tracy McGrady before his undeniable talent led him to star for his high school team in Charlotte, North Carolina. Despite impressive numbers, Curry was overlooked by major schools, so he took his trade to Davidson College, one of the smallest schools in the NCAA I division.

His arrival put the school on the map, and in Curry's first appearance in the NCAA tournament, he dropped 30 points in a loss to fourth-seeded Maryland. The following year, Curry scored 40 against seventh-seeded Gonzaga. The Wildcats then rattled off victories against second-seeded Georgetown and third-seeded Wisconsin before bowing out to the eventual champion, Kansas. Davidson's magical run was over, but Curry had emerged as one to watch. He averaged 28.6 points per game his final year of college before entering the 2009 NBA Draft, where he was selected seventh overall by the Golden State Warriors. Since then, he's amazed with his skill. He finished second in Rookie of the Year voting in 2009–10 and second in the NBA in steals while recording his first triple-double (36 points, 13 assists, 10 rebounds).

Listed at 6-foot-3, Curry's simply become the most dynamic point guard in the game. He already holds the top three spots in the

NBA record books for most threes made in one season (402, 2015–16; 324, 2016–17; 286, 2014–15) and sports a career 44 percent mark from downtown while maintaining a 90 percent free-throw percentage.

There's something special about the way he does it all. Aside from the silky smooth release, his basketball IQ is through the roof. One minute he's running the floor off a steal and dunking with authority; the next he's settling the offense down and dishing no-lookers to a trailing teammate. His bag of tricks includes a killer crossover, a spot-up three, circus shots that seem impossible and a behind-the-back pass that is difficult to intercept. He also had his share of seemingly impossible to hit game-winning baskets, and his ball-handling skills are reinventing the way the game is played.

His highlight-reel season of 2014–15, in which he was named MVP for the first time, included 8 of 11 threes for 40 points, 7 assists and 6 rebounds in a win versus Miami; 34 points, 9 assists, 7 rebounds, 4 steals and 1 block against the Oklahoma Thunder; and an astronomical 10 from beyond the arc in February against Dallas, finishing with 51 points.

He destroyed the competition en route to an NBA Finals berth. Curry did it all, hitting miraculous game-winning shots from the corner, dancing his way to the rim and dropping 30-plus with regularity—including 37 in Game 5 of the finals. The Warriors captured the 2015 NBA Championship, their first in 40 years, and Curry set a playoff record for most threes with 98.

In 2015–16, Curry won his second regular-season MVP award by a unanimous vote and gained entry into the vaunted 50-40-90 club, but he spent most of the 2016 playoffs hurt. The Warriors still returned to the finals but blew the chance to repeat against the Cleveland Cavaliers. Golden State added Kevin Durant in the off-season, and the presence of two MVPs on the same team ensured the Warriors dominated the Western Conference in 2016–17. Early in the season versus New Orleans, Curry dropped 13 — yes, 13 — threes, setting an NBA record.

During the 2017 playoffs, Curry displayed his magic once again. He scored 40 points in Game 1 of the Western Conference finals, hitting seven threes. In Game 2 of the NBA Finals against Cleveland, the point guard notched a triple-double, recording 32 points, 10 rebounds and 11 assists, his first ever trip-dub in the postseason. The Warriors won their second championship in three years, defeating the Cavs in five. Curry dropped 34 points and 10 assists in the deciding game.

The main question about the most creative player in the league, a two-time MVP and holder of two NBA rings, is can anyone stop him?

CAREER HIGHLIGHTS

- Named NBA Most Valuable Player two times (2014–15, 2015–16)
- Has played in four All-Star Games (2014–17)
- NBA scoring champion in 2015–16
- Set the NBA record for three-pointers in a single season (402) in 2015–16
- Active NBA leader in career three-point field goal percentage (.438)

NEW ORLEANS PELICANS

POSITION POWER FORWARD / **SHOOTS** RIGHT / **HEIGHT** 6'11" / **WEIGHT** 253 LB. / **DRAFTED** 2012, NEW ORLEANS HORNETS, 1ST OVERALL

ANTHONY DAVIS 23

THERE'S A NEW superstar emerging in the NBA. He's tall, he's long and he sports the league's most recognizable unibrow. At 6-foot-11 and 253 pounds, Anthony Davis is one of the most talked about young forwards in the league. If he keeps it up, we may be watching a future MVP at work.

Born in 1993, Davis is part of a new youth movement, and at just 24, he appears to be taking his role seriously. The Chicago kid jumped from high school to the University of Kentucky, where he led the Wildcats to a national championship as a freshman in 2012 over the Kansas

Jayhawks. Davis, who routinely set records for blocked shots (including most in one NCAA season), was named MVP of that game after recording 6 points, 16 rebounds, 5 assists, 6 blocks and 3 steals. Former U of K coach Tubby Smith said after the game, "He may be the best player to [ever] play at Kentucky."

His inclusion as a teenager on the 2012 U.S. men's Olympic team signaled he deserved to be mentioned among the elite, and he didn't disappoint in London. At the time, LeBron James said that Davis reminded him of four-time NBA blocks leader Marcus Camby. Kobe Bryant resolved to mentor the 19-year-old after seeing him finish alley-oops from Kevin Durant and Chris Paul. His length, defensive awareness and energy impressed the group of future Hall of Famers. It was a coming-out party for the first overall pick.

In his first full season playing for the New Orleans Hornets (2012–13), Davis played 64 games, averaging 13.5 points per game, 8.2 rebounds and 1.8 blocks despite several injury scares, including a concussion and a sprained knee. He managed to impress league-wide, posting 28 points and 11 rebounds versus Milwaukee early in the season, and consistently began dropping double-doubles in the second half. "Fear the Brow" became a household phrase.

The following year the team name changed to the Pelicans, and it proved positive. Davis clearly focused on the little

ally drove defenses mad with his ruthless combo of size and touch. At the end of January, he was on pace for the greatest player efficiency rating (PER) in the history of the NBA. He finished with a mark of 30.81. The only two players since 1973–74 (when the NBA began tracking individual turnovers) to have posted higher ratings? Michael Jordan and LeBron James. Pretty heady company.

If he's not making a deft post move, Davis is hitting nothing but net from 15 feet out. He can dribble like a guard (he started as one in high school before springing to 6-foot-11) or drop back for a three and run the court with elegance and power. And of course, there's that 7-foot-5 wingspan.

His offensive output in 2015–16 was equally devastating, despite his missing over 20 games at the end of the year due to lingering shoulder and knee injuries — he finished the season with 24.3 points and 10.3 assists. He matched Shaquille O'Neal and Chris Webber as the only NBA players since 1983 to post a 50-point, 20-rebound game: he went off for 59 and 22 versus Detroit in February 2016, establishing a new franchise record for points scored in a game.

And Davis just keeps getting better. In 2016–17 he was named to the All-NBA First Team for the second time. His opening game was nothing short of miraculous — 50 points, 16 rebounds and 7 steals. Later in the season, he went off for 46 points and 21 rebounds versus Charlotte. He continued dominating opponents and increased his season totals to 28 points a night — including 11.8 off the glass — 2.2 blocks and an 80 percent free-throw percentage. The addition of DeMarcus Cousins at the 2017 trade deadline means New Orleans now has the most dominant front court in the league.

It's a foregone conclusion that Davis will be a perennial All-Star. The question many are asking is how many trophies will this guy win?

CAREER HIGHLIGHTS

- Named an NBA All-Rookie (First Team) in 2012–13
- Named the All-Star Game MVP in 2017
- Has played in four All-Star Games (2014–2017)
- Is a two-time All-NBA First Team selection (2014–15, 2016–17)
- Led the league in blocks per game in 2013–14 (2.8) and 2014–15 (2.9)

things that off-season, and he saw his totals increase. He nearly doubled his trips to the line and increased his free-throw percentage to .791 — impressive for a big man. He finished with 20.8 points per game (an increase of nearly 7 points), 10 rebounds and 2.8 blocks in 67 games.

His 2014–15 NBA campaign got off to a blistering start. He dropped an opening night for the ages: 26 points, 17 rebounds, 9 blocks, 3 steals and 2 assists — results not seen since the likes of another big man, Hakeem Olajuwon. Davis continu-

GOLDEN STATE WARRIORS

POSITION SMALL FORWARD / **SHOOTS** RIGHT / **HEIGHT** 6'9" / **WEIGHT** 240 LB. / **DRAFTED** 2007, SEATTLE SUPERSONICS, 2ND OVERALL

KEVIN DURANT 35

PURE, UNADULTERATED TALENT. That's what you see when watching Kevin Durant play. He oozes talent and flashes brilliance, all while maintaining a humble, low-key personality that's made him into one of the great heirs to the modern basketball throne.

Durant grew up in Seat Pleasant, on the outskirts of Washington, D.C., where his mother worked long shifts hauling 70-pound mailbags for the postal service. Gangly, he entered an elementary school gym and quickly learned the game under the supervision of a life-changing mentor nicknamed Chucky, who was shot to death when Durant was in high school. To honor his mentor, the future NBA superstar chose to wear the number 35, Chucky's age when he died. Chucky's death hardened the shy Durant, and he immersed himself in basketball.

He played just one season at the University of Texas at Austin, averaging 25.8 points, and was drafted to the NBA second overall in 2007 behind Greg Oden. Durant saw his not going first overall as a slight, and it took him a decade to shed the feeling of second best.

The Seattle SuperSonics, who became the Oklahoma City Thunder in 2008, won only 20 games with their fresh

draft choice in the backcourt in 2007–08. Durant was skinny, shot the ball too much and had a poor diet. His game appeared one-dimensional, and he was nicknamed "Starvin' Marvin."

The team moved to Oklahoma and everything changed. Durant was always in the gym, always shooting, always leading by example. His coach at the time, Scott Brooks, called him "good boring." Despite a 3-29 start, Oklahoma won 20 of their last 30, and change was in the air.

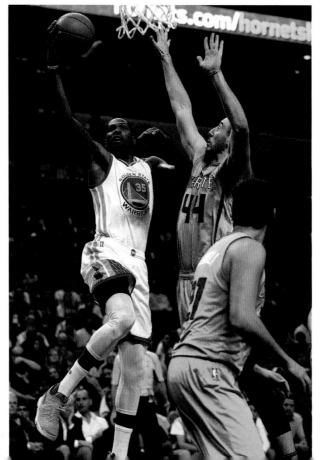

In 2009–10, Durant won the scoring title at 21 years of age, the youngest ever to do so. He continued dominating the league, leading Oklahoma to the Western Conference finals in 2011 and the NBA Finals the following season, falling 4-1 to the LeBron James–led Miami Heat.

Durant scorched the NBA for a career-high 32 points per game as well as 7.4 rebounds and 5.5 assists during his MVP season in 2013–14, punctuated by his heart-wrenching acceptance speech where he thanked his mom by saying, "You're the real MVP." Diagnosed with a chronic foot problem in the summer after his MVP season, Durant needed three separate surgeries to repair a fracture in his right foot. In 2014–15 he played only 27 games and the Thunder missed the playoffs. The big positive from the lost season was the revelation of teammate Russell Westbrook, who dominated the league and finished as the scoring leader.

With Durant averaging 28.2 points and 8.2 rebounds during the 2015–16 season, the Thunder went all the way to Game 7 of the 2016 Western Conference finals. In Game 6 in Oklahoma, Durant had been just five minutes away from a second berth in the NBA Finals when Golden State Warrior

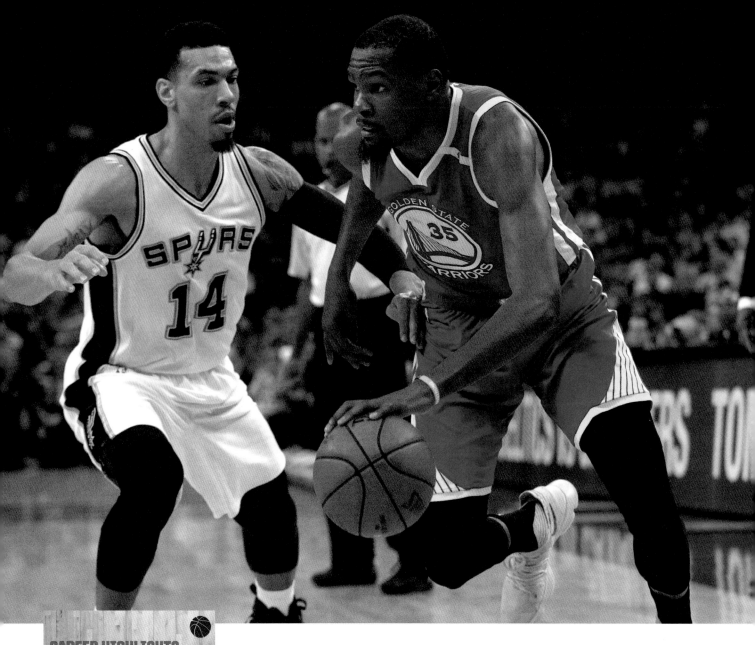

- Named NBA Most Valuable Player for 2013–14
- Named MVP of the NBA Finals in 2017
- Named NBA Rookie of the Year for 2007–08
- Named the All-Star Game MVP in 2012
- Is a five-time All-NBA First Team selection (2009–10 to 2013–14)

sharpshooter Klay Thompson hit 11 three-pointers and cued a fourth-quarter come-back that signaled Durant's final home game for the franchise that drafted him.

Everyone, including Durant, knew he needed to start winning championships to secure his legacy. Sensing Oklahoma had peaked, he elected to join the Warriors as a free agent, joining a powerhouse team that went 67-15 and won their first 15 games in the playoffs. Durant averaged 25.1 points, 8.3 rebounds and 4.8 dimes over the regular season despite missing 20 games with a knee injury. He and Steph Curry formed a one-two punch that proved nearly impossible to match as the Warriors lost just once down the stretch and once in the postseason.

That playoff run would go a long way to change the minds of Durant's doubters.

Durant played some of the best basketball of his career. The forward led all scorers in Game 1 of the NBA Finals with 38 points. The following game, he posted a game-high 33, adding 13 rebounds, 6 assists, 5 blocks and 3 steals — an all-around game that had tongues wagging. He capped off the five-game series with a 39-point performance in Game 5, winning his first championship ring. Durant was named finals MVP, and when asked postgame to say something about his mom, he simply said, "We did it."

At 29 years old, the four-time scoring champion is the purest, most natural scorer in the NBA. No one doubts the talent. No one doubts the numbers. And now with a championship title, Durant may finally have entered the conversation as one of the greatest players of his generation.

HOUSTON ROCKETS

POSITION SHOOTING GUARD / **SHOOTS** LEFT / **HEIGHT** 6'5" / **WEIGHT** 220 LB. / **DRAFTED** 2009, OKLAHOMA CITY THUNDER, 3RD OVERALL

JAMES HARDEN 13

JAMES HARDEN IS hard to miss. He's more beard than ball, more flash than pan. Coming to the NBA via Arizona State as the third overall pick in 2009, Harden's become one of the league's true superstars. Thanks to his myriad skills as well as his bushy, hard-to-miss chin, he's propelling the Houston Rockets to the top of the NBA class.

Harden was born in Bellflower, California, and he played ball at the same Los Angeles high school as former NBA players the O'Bannon brothers and Jason Kapono. A myth pervaded that Harden's first coach deemed him an NBA star upon first sight, but in 2012 he said simply that he could tell Harden "was going to be a good high school player." What's unmistakable is the guard had gifts early on, and his Artesia High team won two state championships before he accepted a scholarship to Arizona State.

Taken third by the Oklahoma Thunder, Harden found himself outside the starting five on a stacked young franchise that included Kevin Durant and Russell Westbrook. The circumstance wasn't one that spelled certain stardom. No matter, Harden made his case as best he could.

In the 2011–12 season, a coming-out year for the bearded wonder, he was named Sixth Man of the Year, the youngest in history. Harden's presence off the bench was a massive factor in the Thunder's reaching the NBA Finals that season. A .491 shooting percentage, coupled with 39 percent from behind the arc, meant All-Star-level production coming off the bench for Oklahoma. Problem was, after a finals loss to the Miami Heat, there was simply no way Oklahoma could keep Harden as well as future MVPs Durant and Westbrook. Unable to offer Harden the "franchise player" money he deserved heading into the 2012–13 season, the Thunder dealt the talented guard to the Rockets, where he's become the backbone of the team and the centerpiece for an offense that relies heavily on the three-point shot.

What did Harden do once he got to Houston? He started with a first game for

the ages: 37 points, 12 assists, 6 rebounds and 4 steals. He continued his stellar play and made his first All-Star appearance. He posted a 45-point night and his first triple-double and finished the year as the fifth highest scorer in the NBA (25.9 points per game). And all this after helping Team USA to Olympic gold in 2012. Was he worth $80 million over five years? It certainly looked like it.

Following the addition of Dwight Howard the Rockets soared in the regular season, finishing 2013–14 with a 54-28 record. But matched against the Damian Lillard–led Portland Trail Blazers, the Rockets lost a heartbreaker of a Game 6 in the first round of the playoffs when Lillard dropped a buzzer-beating three to end the series. Harden averaged 27 points per game in the losing effort.

Harden doesn't just score, he impacts the entire game when he's on the court. Using his lethal Eurostep, the left-handed dribbler drives to the basket, where he's one of the NBA's top players in drawing fouls. It doesn't hurt that he's an 85 percent free-throw shooter. And now that he's one of the league's top assists men, he's made defenders worry about something more than his speed to the basket and his killer crossover. The 2014–15 season was good to Harden. He led the league in total points (2,217), and he finished second in points per game (27.37) and first in free throws made and attempted. He finished ninth overall in

assists per game (6.98), despite mostly playing shooting guard. He increased his rebounds, steals and blocks per game and established himself as an MVP candidate, finishing second overall in voting.

But 2015–16 was a different story. The Rockets finished 41-41 and were bounced from the playoffs in the first round by the Golden State Warriors despite Harden's starring role as one-man wrecking crew. The following season he started demolishing the record books. He put up 22 triple-doubles, which included a never-before-seen 53 points, 17 assists and 16 rebounds versus the Knicks. If not for Russell Westbrook's own onslaught of the

record books, Harden would have been a sure lock for MVP. Quite simply, he did it all in Houston, finishing the year with 29.1 points, 11.2 assists and 8.1 rebounds, and despite the Rockets' second-round loss to the San Antonio Spurs, Harden reestablished Houston as a strong contender in the Western Conference.

The gregarious guard, whose beard has its own Twitter account, is thriving with the weight of the Rockets' offense on his shoulders. In just a few short years he's become one of the best players in the world, and if he brings a championship to Houston, he'll live on with Rockets legends like Moses Malone and Hakeem Olajuwon.

POSITION SMALL FORWARD / **SHOOTS** RIGHT / **HEIGHT** 6'8" / **WEIGHT** 250 LB. / **DRAFTED** 2003, CLEVELAND CAVALIERS, 1ST OVERALL

LEBRON JAMES 23

FEW BASKETBALL PLAYERS define an era. But when they do, they're often known by a single name. Kareem. Bird. Magic. Jordan. And the man who has ushered basketball into the 21st century is known simply as LeBron.

LeBron James was born in 1984 in Akron, Ohio. By his junior year of high school, he was the most famous teen athlete in the United States, appearing on the cover of Sports Illustrated and wowing the nation with his unique blend of size, speed and athleticism. When the Cleveland Cavaliers made him the number one overall pick in the 2003 NBA Draft, he was already more famous than Bird, Magic or Jordan were at that stage in their careers. One writer called James "the most hyped basketball player ever."

Football-player big at 6-foot-8 and 250 pounds, James immediately made an impact on the NBA as an 18-year-old in 2003–04, dropping 25 points in his first game. James was the automatic choice for Rookie of the Year, and in his second season, LeBron started making magic, scorching the Toronto Raptors for 56 points and posting four games of 40 points or more and 22 games with 30 points or more — astonishing numbers for a 20-year-old.

Despite being the league's leading scorer in 2007–08 with 30 points per game, LeBron bettered himself during the 2008–09 season. He led the Cavs in the five major statistical categories en route to a 66-16

record. But a third-round exit at the hands of the Orlando Magic ruined hopes of a title to cap off his MVP-winning year. Lack of success in Cleveland weighed on James. Opting out of his contract with Cleveland and signing with the Miami Heat for the 2010–11 season allowed James to form a mini-dynasty with Chris Bosh and Dwyane Wade, his fellow 2003 draftees.

In terms of legacy making, he accomplished his goal, reaching the finals four times in a row during his tenure with the Heat, winning twice, and twice more he was named MVP to go along with the two he earned in Cleveland. But with an opt-out clause, James controlled his own destiny, choosing to return to Cleveland in 2014–15 as the prodigal son.

Everyone wondered if the fans would embrace him — they burned his jersey when he first turned his back on the city. But success has a funny way of changing things. With Kyrie Irving and Kevin Love as his new right-hand men, LeBron began eyeing the next challenge. After a sluggish start for Cleveland's new trio, the Cavaliers finally found their rhythm, coasting to a 53-29 record. LeBron finished the year averaging 25.3 points, 6 rebounds and 7.4 assists.

He one-upped even himself in the playoffs. Missing Love to injury during the second round, the Cavs dispatched the Bulls in six games with LeBron averaging 26 points, 11 boards and 8.8 assists over the series. Cleveland then coasted past the Hawks, and by Game 1 of the finals against the Golden State Warriors, it was just LeBron and a cast of secondary characters after Irving succumbed to a broken kneecap.

He scored 44 in a Game 1 loss and recorded a triple-double in Game 2, both of which went to overtime. In a Game 5 loss, he recorded a 40-point triple-double. James finished the series averaging 35.8 points, 13.3 rebounds and 8.8 assists, the first player in finals history to lead both teams in all major statistical categories.

In 2016, he brought Cleveland its first title in fifty-plus years, climbing back from a 3-1 series deficit in a rematch versus Golden State. James was named finals MVP that year and will forever be remembered for "the Block," a full-court chase-down of Andre Iguodala in the final minutes of Game 7 that helped secure the championship.

LeBron is a 13-time All-Star, four-time MVP, three-time finals MVP and three-time Olympic medalist. His career numbers

- Named NBA Most Valuable Player four times (2008–09, 2009–10, 2011–12, 2012–13)
- Named MVP of the NBA Finals three times (2012, 2013, 2016)
- Named the All-Star Game MVP two times (2006, 2008)
- Has played in 13 All-Star Games (2005–2017)
- Won an Olympic gold medal with the U.S. men's basketball team in Beijing in 2008 and London in 2012

undoubtedly put him in the upper echelon of anyone who has ever played the game of basketball. He cracked the top 10 all-time scoring list in 2016–17 and may be the only man on the planet to have a shot at dethroning Kareem Abdul-Jabbar's record. In 2017 he set the all-time playoff scoring record, eclipsing Michael Jordan, and became the first player to average a triple-double in the NBA Finals despite losing to the Warriors in five games. He may not be the purest scorer, strongest rebounder or most efficient playmaker, but the man who has already been to eight NBA Finals may go down as the most complete basketball player the world has ever seen.

POSITION SMALL FORWARD / **SHOOTS** RIGHT / **HEIGHT** 6'7" / **WEIGHT** 230 LB. / **DRAFTED** 2011, INDIANA PACERS, 15TH OVERALL

KAWHI LEONARD [2]

KAWHI LEONARD BARELY registered on the radar when he first entered the league. Now, he's the most valuable player for the San Antonio Spurs and was top five in the 2017 MVP voting, adding to a list of accolades that includes being named the MVP of the 2014 NBA Finals and the league's best defensive player the following year.

He's an unassuming 6-foot-7, if that's even possible. The 15th overall pick in the 2011 draft, Leonard was traded by the Indiana Pacers to San Antonio, where he's been a revelation; his being plucked by the Spurs is another moment of talent evaluation by the franchise that has paid great dividends.

Leonard's two years at San Diego State were solid, and in his second and final season, he took the Aztecs all the way to the Sweet 16. That season he threw up averages of 15.9 points and 10.6 rebounds. But Leonard hasn't had the easiest route. His father was killed outside the car wash he owned in Compton in 2008 while Kawhi was in high school. Leonard grew up there washing cars and learned a work ethic that transferred to the court. The tragedy instilled a quiet toughness in his personality, and his agent called Leonard "the most dedicated guy I've ever been around."

In 2013–14, en route to his first championship and first finals MVP award, Leonard contributed 12.8 points and 6.2 boards to the Spurs' attack during the regular season. His presence rounded out a formidably deep group intent on proving that age ain't nothin' but a number — with veterans like Tim Duncan, Tony Parker and Manu Ginobili showing the young Leonard how to win. Despite a slow start that saw him net only 9 points in each of the first two games of the finals, he exploded in Game 3 and was golden the rest of the way, averaging 23.7 points and 9.3 rebounds in the last three games of the series as the Spurs closed out the Miami Heat in five.

In 2014–15 Leonard averaged 16.5 points, 7.2 rebounds and 2.5 assists in

31.8 minutes per game despite missing 18 games midseason to injury. He also led the league in steals per game (2.3). Basically, he's been the engine of the team, emerging from the shadows to lead the aging Spurs superstars when needed. He's a presence on both ends of the floor, and his point production increased by four per game over the previous season even as he was named the best defensive player in the league. But perhaps because he was the young gun on a team of All-Stars, Leonard's contributions were overlooked. Or perhaps it's his low-key personality and humility, especially since the loss of his father. But that's all changed now. The Spurs are Leonard's team going forward. The international trifecta that nurtured him has already started sailing into the sunset, and the small forward has been called on to carry the team.

In 2015–16 Leonard averaged 21.2 points a game while maintaining his status as the top shutdown defender in the league.

The Spurs went 67-15 in Duncan's final season, but it was Leonard, named a starter for the first time in the 2016 All-Star Game, who garnered all the attention.

During the 2016–17 regular season Leonard put up 25.5, the highest total of his career. He also shot 88 percent from the line, hit 38 percent from deep and led the Spurs back to the Western Conference finals before an ankle injury sidelined him. The injury effectively dashed San Antonio's hopes of dethroning the Golden State Warriors, who made their third straight NBA Finals appearance.

Where Leonard really excels is in shutting down his opponent's best players — making long nights out of games for the league's top stars. He's simply too much of everything all at once: he's too big for some, too long for others, too quick for many and too tenacious on and off the ball for most. (His hands are also massive, 11.25 inches from pinkie to thumb, more than 50 percent larger than the average person and reminiscent of another top defender, Hall of Famer Scottie Pippen.)

The Spurs — despite winning five championships since 1999 — have never registered back-to-back titles. Leonard's only 26 years old, but with the wisdom passed on from the NBA's elder statesmen, he'll be ready to change that. Just wait.

- Named MVP of the NBA Finals in 2014
- Named NBA Defensive Player of the Year two times (2014–15, 2015–16)
- Named to NBA All-Defensive First Team two times (2015, 2016)
- Has played in two All-Star Games (2016, 2017)
- Is a two-time All-NBA First Team selection (2015–16, 2016–17)

HOUSTON ROCKETS

POSITION POINT GUARD / **SHOOTS** RIGHT / **HEIGHT** 6'0" / **WEIGHT** 175 LB. / **DRAFTED** 2005, NEW ORLEANS HORNETS, 4TH OVERALL

CHRIS PAUL 99

IF YOU WANT a smooth, pure basketball player who makes playing in the NBA look easy and is a true gentleman on and off the court, look no further than Chris Paul.

Ever since winning Rookie of the Year for his stellar 2005–06 campaign, there has been no stopping the ascent of the 6-foot guard. He's a team leader whose effusive charm, wide smile and hustle on the court have earned him accolades as one of the most respected players in the league.

The product of Wake Forest, Paul spent two years running the floor for the Demon Deacons, averaging 15 points and 6.3 assists per game before declaring for the 2005 draft, where he was taken fourth overall by the New Orleans Hornets.

It wasn't until his third year (2007–08) that Paul led the Hornets to the playoffs, and that season he exceeded the already high expectations placed on him. Paul led the NBA in assists (925), assists per game (11.6), steals (217) and steals per game (2.7) while knocking down 21.1 points per contest. His dominance on both ends of the floor had him second in MVP voting to the LA Lakers' Kobe Bryant. The Hornets also won their only playoff series to date that year, a 4-1 romp over the Dallas Mavericks in which Paul destroyed Jason Kidd in their 1-on-1 matchup, while recording three double-doubles in the series and a triple-double in the final game.

But Paul's time with the Hornets was short-lived. With no supporting cast,

and not wanting to play in the basement, he asked to be dealt, leading to the most famous NBA trade that never happened. Commissioner David Stern, in a completely unprecedented move, vetoed a deal that would have sent Paul to the Lakers to join Kobe Bryant, a dream scenario that never

manifested. Days later, Paul was shipped to the Clippers. There, he teamed with Blake Griffin to form a duo equally formidable to the Paul–Bryant pipe dream.

Paul's a perennial leader in the assist category. Four times he's led the league, including back-to-back seasons of 10-plus

assists per game in 2013–14 and 2014–15. He's a dish-first point guard who looks for backdoor cuts, trailing big men or plays off the pick and roll. But don't mistake him for an average shooter — he's lethal with an open-look jumper. Paul is creative off the dribble, possesses a killer crossover and, when he was in LA, developed an out-of-this world aerial chemistry with the super-talented Griffin. The Clippers' nickname, "Lob City," didn't come about by accident.

And what's become apparent is that Paul may be best as a Robin, not a Batman. He's still a strong court general — always probing new ways to the basket, posing as a threat to pass, shoot, lob or penetrate deep into the key. He is solid on D too. Paul has six times led the league in steals, including four straight (2010–11 to 2013–14). He is still arguably one of the best defensive point guards in the NBA, and he continues to put up a couple of steals per contest.

Where Paul's critics slam him is in the postseason. But given his virtuoso performance in Game 7 of the first round of the 2015 playoffs against the San Antonio Spurs, that tune started to change. Fighting through a hamstring injury, Paul drove to the hoop and hit a last-second off-balance, off-the glass winner to send the Clips to the next round. It was easily the biggest shot of his career and silenced those who claimed Paul isn't clutch. The Clips still managed to blow a 3-1 lead in the second round to the Houston Rockets, and Paul, despite playing his guts out, failed once again to reach a conference finals.

He put up 19.5 points and 10 dimes the following season, but ever judged on his postseason success, the year was deemed a disappointment when Paul broke his hand in the first round against Portland and the Clippers exited early. The point guard had some serious stat lines in 2016–17, none greater than his 20 points and 20 assists (and zero turnovers) in a 133–105 win versus New Orleans — the first time in 32 years a player has accomplished that feat. In the 2017 playoffs, the Clippers fell to the Utah Jazz in seven games despite

Paul's averaging 25 points, 10 assists and 5 rebounds over the seven-game series. All signs pointed to the franchise giving him a new contract, but in June 2017, Paul was traded to the Houston Rockets for seven players and a 2018 draft pick.

Paul has already cracked the top 10 in all-time assists and will likely go down not only as the greatest point guard of his generation but as one of the best to ever grace the floor. For Paul, only a championship, perhaps with his new Houston squad, will burnish his legacy further.

CAREER HIGHLIGHTS

- Named NBA Rookie of the Year for 2005–06
- Named the All-Star Game MVP in 2013
- Is a four-time All-NBA First Team selection (2008, 2012–2014)
- Is the active NBA assist-per-game leader (9.9)
- Won an Olympic gold medal with the U.S. men's basketball team in Beijing in 2008 and London in 2012

POSITION SHOOTING GUARD / **SHOOTS** RIGHT / **HEIGHT** 6'4" / **WEIGHT** 220 LB. / **DRAFTED** 2003, MIAMI HEAT, 5TH OVERALL

DWYANE WADE [3]

FEW GUARDS IN recent memory have had an impact on the game like Dwyane Wade. A slasher, a shooter, a leader, Wade's combined attributes have made him what all athletes aspire to be called: a winner.

He didn't have the easiest upbringing on the South Side of Chicago, with a mother in and out of jail and suffering from addiction issues. He turned to sports, thriving on both the basketball court and the football field. In his senior year, he dropped a cool 27 points and 11 rebounds on average as a starting shooting guard for Harold L. Richards High School in Oak Lawn, Illinois.

Wade spent two years at Marquette before leapfrogging to the NBA. He was drafted fifth overall in the 2003 draft, which was one of the best on record; the draft included his future teammates LeBron James and Chris Bosh. At Marquette, he was an absolute stud, averaging 19.7 points a game and racking up 150 steals and 79 blocked shots over two seasons. But the highlight was his triple-double (only the fourth in NCAA history at that point) against number one ranked Kentucky in the 2003 NCAA tournament, vaulting Marquette into the Final Four for the first time since 1977.

"D-Wade" spent most of his career in Miami, winning three titles. But perhaps the first one is the most memorable — it certainly marked Wade's arrival as a bona fide superstar. In just his third season,

CAREER HIGHLIGHTS

- Named MVP of the NBA Finals in 2006
- Named the All-Star Game MVP in 2010
- Has played in 12 All-Star Games (2005–2016)
- Was the NBA scoring champion in 2008–09
- Won an Olympic gold medal with the U.S. men's basketball team in Beijing in 2008

Wade dropped 27.2 points a game in the regular season, adding 6.7 assists and 5.7 rebounds, some serious numbers from the 2-guard position. The Heat soared through the playoffs but found themselves down 0-2 in the finals to Dirk Nowitzki and the Dallas Mavericks. The Heat fought back, winning four straight. Wade dropped over 40 points in both Games 3 and 5, battling through injuries, and he was named 2006 finals MVP.

Wade missed large chunks of the next two seasons with injuries, but he still managed to help the 2008 men's U.S. Olympic team win gold in Beijing. But once healthy again, he dominated the NBA. In the 2008–09 season, he led the NBA in scoring, putting up 30.2 points per game. But the Heat were ousted in seven against the Hawks, and things were about to change.

Wade's career with the Heat turned a corner when he helped persuade James and Bosh to leave their respective teams and join him in Miami. All three belonged to the same draft class and thus had expiring contracts. The move tipped the balance of players' working contracts to their favor rather than general managers always dictating the terms.

The trio formed an unstoppable presence in South Beach, making four trips in a row to the NBA Finals, winning twice. It wasn't the multiple rings that James boasted they would win when they announced their decision in 2010, but it was enough for the rest of the league to take notice — the Heat were the team to beat for four years, and in the modern cap era, as close to a dynasty as it gets.

Wade and Bosh remained in Miami for the 2014–15 season, bidding adieu to LeBron, who returned to Cleveland. But Bosh and Wade, who amassed major playoff minutes over the years, were hampered by injuries, and the Heat failed to make the playoffs despite stalwart efforts by both. Wade for his part averaged 21.5 points in 62 games, adding 4.8 assists and 3.5 off the glass. The following season, he willed the Heat to Game 7 of the second round of the playoffs. Miami eventually fell to the Toronto Raptors, but Wade's performance — he shot a stunning 52.2 percent from beyond the arc in 14 games — proved he still had MVP buried in his DNA.

In 2016–17 Wade landed in his hometown of Chicago, where he provided veteran star power to the Bulls squad. Although Wade may have some miles, the shooting guard isn't quite resigned to a backup veteran role just yet. He started 59 of 60 games for the Bulls and chipped in 18.3 points in 30 minutes of work a night — solid numbers for a guy in his fourteenth season. He can still drive to the basket and nail his off-balance shots; he can still cross over and pull up for the J; and his mere presence on the court is enough to make a young guard quiver on the defensive end.

He's one of the league's good guys — off the court he's a role model who is active in charitable events. And with three rings, he's proven that he's not only a winner but a fighter, too; he's won as top dog and as a supporting star. He's a classic example of a team-first superstar.

OKLAHOMA CITY THUNDER

POSITION POINT GUARD / **SHOOTS** RIGHT / **HEIGHT** 6'3" / **WEIGHT** 200 LB. / **DRAFTED** 2008, SEATTLE SUPERSONICS, 4TH OVERALL

RUSSELL WESTBROOK [0]

IT WAS HARD to tell what the Oklahoma City Thunder (formerly the Seattle SuperSonics) acquired with the fourth overall pick in the 2008 draft when they selected Russell Westbrook. He didn't shine in high school until his senior year, when he averaged 25.1 points per game and grabbed 8.7 rebounds as a point guard for Leuzinger High School in Long Beach, California. One thing was certain though: he made his basketball teams better. Twice, UCLA made the Final Four with Westbrook in the backcourt, and during his last year before declaring for the NBA Draft he posted 12.7 points, 3.7 rebounds and 4.9 assists. But was that any indicator he would become one of the most feared men in the NBA?

His first coach certainly knew, commenting in 2011 upon Westbrook's first All-Star Game: "Russell . . . had a vision at a young age of what he wanted to do and where he wanted to get." His father, Russell Sr., also knew — or at least ensured a strong work ethic that would become the backbone of Westbrook's game, as the protégé would take 500 shots per day and do countless sit-ups and push-ups. Despite being undersized, Westbrook had a reputation for being the toughest and hardest-working player on the court.

That work ethic continued when he arrived in Oklahoma, joining heralded small forward Kevin Durant to form one of the NBA's best one-two combos. But Westbrook began largely in Durant's shadow. It's no slight — Durant is a former MVP, a four-time scoring champ and an eight-time All-Star. So for Westbrook to become as formidable a force as Durant is incredible.

His rookie season, Westbrook put home a solid 15.1 points per game, along with 4.9 rebounds, 5.3 assists and 1.3 steals. By his third year, he'd increased almost every one of those totals en route to a first All-Star appearance — 21.9 points, 4.6 rebounds, 8.2 assists and nearly 2 steals per game. That season he helped lead

- Named NBA Most Valuable Player for 2016–17
- Named the All-Star Game MVP two times (2015, 2016)
- Has played in six All-Star Games (2011–13, 2015–17)
- Is a two-time All-NBA First Team selection (2015–16, 2016–17)
- Led the NBA in points per game in 2014–15 (28.1) and 2016–17 (31.6)

25-19-11 line days later against the Clippers. He capped the season with the second most steals and the second most assists, and he finished eighth in scoring.

Westbrook and Durant took Oklahoma all the way to Game 7 of the 2016 conference finals but bowed out to the Warriors. Westbrook, for his part, posted double digits in assists in six of seven games and contributed 26 points and 11 assists a game over 18 playoff games, a slight improvement on his regular-season numbers.

Durant bolted to Golden State when free agency beckoned, leaving Westbrook to helm the Thunder. Quite simply, the point guard put up the most dominant offensive season in the NBA since 1961–62, when Oscar Robertson averaged a triple-double for the entire season. Westbrook's season-average 31.6 points, 10.4 assists and 10.7 rebounds were out of this world. In a late-season game he notched 57 points, 13 rebounds and 11 assists, the highest point total for any triple-double in NBA history. Westbrook finished the season with 42 triple-doubles — an NBA record and the signature on his MVP season.

If anyone is going to ensure a trip back to the playoffs for Oklahoma, it's the hard-working point guard from Long Beach. No longer in the shadow of Durant, this MVP is making a case that it may have been his team all along.

the Thunder to their first NBA Finals appearance — losing in five games to the Miami Heat. In 2013–14, Westbrook shone in the playoffs despite Oklahoma's loss in the conference finals to the San Antonio Spurs. He absolutely commanded the floor, averaging a whopping 26.7 points, 8.1 rebounds and 7.3 assists during the series.

He's one of the most versatile point guards in the game. He can hurt opposing teams in a variety of ways, whether by attacking the hoop, dropping a 15-footer — his "cotton shot" — or passing to a cutting big man like Stephen Adams. Although Westbrook may not be a reliable three-point threat, his tough-as-nails defense makes up for his lack of deep scoring.

The Thunder hit a speed bump in 2014–15. Durant suffered a broken foot during the preseason and Westbrook followed with a broken hand several games in — the team was behind the eight ball from the get-go. But a turning point came in mid-December versus the Cleveland Cavaliers. With Westbrook and Durant both finally back, they combined for 45 points and it finally felt like the old championship-caliber Thunder. Over a four-game stretch, Westbrook became the first player since Michael Jordan to post four straight triple-doubles.

In 2015–16, Westbrook registered back-to-back 40-point games early in the season, heaved up 44 points versus the Pelicans after the All-Star break and recorded a

THE NBA DRAFT

BOOM OR BUST IN '84

In 1984, the Portland Trail Blazers selected Sam Bowie second overall, one spot behind Hakeem "the Dream" Olajuwon and one position ahead of a guard from North Carolina named Michael Jordan. In hindsight, how anyone could pass up the greatest basketball player of all time may seem baffling, almost unconscionable. It's why to this day the 1984 draft is the most scrutinized, perhaps the most famous draft class of all time. That's not because of Jordan — it's because of Bowie.

At the time, Jordan's going third made sense. Guards were not seen as focal points of basketball teams in the 70s and 80s — big men like Bill Walton, Julius Erving and Kareem Abdul-Jabbar were — and players like Jordan and Magic Johnson had yet to make a full impact on the psyche of executives and fans during the 80s. The 1984 draft in many ways became a tipping point for a new NBA.

A series of unusual circumstances sent Bowie — the greatest high school player of his era — to Portland. The Trail Blazers selected

Sam Bowie, left, and Hakeem Olajuwon flank NBA commissioner David Stern following the 1984 draft.

33

future All-Star Clyde Drexler at the guard position in 1983 — he declared before his senior year to enter the '83 draft — so with no need for another backcourt presence, Portland had set their sights beyond Jordan well before the executives gathered in Madison Square Garden for the '84 draft.

Portland, well aware of Bowie's progress, and unhappy with their center Tom Owens, traded the underperforming big to Indiana in June of 1981 in exchange for Indiana's number one pick in '84. Luckily for Portland, the Pacers finished dead last in the East in 1983–84, positioning the Blazers in what became a two-horse race for a game-changing player with the West's worst team, the Houston Rockets. The fate of both franchises came down to a simple coin toss for the number one pick (the draft lottery didn't begin until 1985).

Houston won the flip, and as they say, the rest is history.

By choosing Olajuwon, Drexler's college teammate in Houston, the Rockets got an immensely talented Nigerian-born center who'd taken his college team to back-to-back NCAA finals. Portland's consolation prize was Bowie. The Trail Blazers' prior success with another pass-heavy big man, Bill Walton, weighed heavily in the minds of management prior to the 1984 draft. They needed a center to complement Drexler, not another guard. So they chose big, passing over Jordan.

The debate still rages: do you take the most talented player in the draft, regardless of position, or do you fill a need? Mind you, if Bowie hadn't been injured in college, redshirted and played an extra fifth year, he might have gone number one in '83, and the whole Jordan fiasco would have been prevented. (Olajuwon also redshirted a year upon arrival in the U.S.) Another NBA-ready center, Patrick Ewing, who defeated Olajuwon in the 1984 NCAA finals, remained for his senior season at Georgetown. Drafted first overall in 1985, imagine how insane a draft with Ewing, Bowie, and Olajuwon would have been. Hindsight is 20/20, but one wonders if Bowie's career trajectory would have been different as well if Drexler hadn't declared early and Ewing hadn't declared late. An even greater urban myth (at least according to Olajuwon's autobiography) persists that Portland nearly traded Drexler and the second overall pick to Houston for Ralph Sampson. Meaning the Rockets would have ended up with Jordan, Drexler and Olajuwon — one of those three played in an NBA Finals every season from 1990 to 1998 with their respective teams.

WHO WAS SAM Bowie, and how did he become the biggest bust of all time? A 7-foot-1 high school phenom from Lebanon, Pennsylvania, Bowie, as a junior, took his team all the way to the state final before losing by one point. In his senior year in 1979 he averaged 28.8 points per game. Few centers his size could run the floor with grace and agility at such a young age; few could pass like a guard and post

Sam Bowie of Kentucky hauls down a rebound against Georgetown in the 1984 NCAA tournament.

like a big. Bowie was so legendary in high school, he signed autographs everywhere he went with the signature "the Million Dollar Kid." His face was plastered on the cover of sports sections across the country, including the cover of *Sports Illustrated*. For a time, it's not an overstatement to say that Bowie was the most famous basketball player on the planet. Four hundred colleges contacted the teenager — he eventually chose the University of Kentucky. But injuries in college caused Bowie to miss nearly two years of basketball after a broken leg was left untreated and never healed properly. By the time he reached the NBA Draft in 1984, moments away from realizing his lifelong dream and cashing in big time, he had buckled under the pressure. In 2012, for an ESPN documentary, Bowie revealed he lied to the Trail Blazers about the pain in his leg prior to the draft. When the Portland medical team tapped on his tibia during a physical, Bowie said, "I can still remember them taking a little mallet, and when they would hit me on my left tibia . . . I would tell 'em, 'I don't feel anything.' But deep down inside, it was hurting." Desperate to achieve his NBA dream, he went on to say he did what anyone would have done in his position, and one can't help but look back tragically at a man hanging on to a fading dream.

A 17-year-old Kobe Bryant is all smiles after the post-draft trade that sent him from Charlotte to Los Angeles.

Inexplicably, Portland factored into another great draft bust, Greg Oden. Taken first overall by the Trail Blazers in 2007, Oden, who recently retired, was injured most of his career and never made an impact for any team. Even worse, the Blazers could have had Kevin Durant that year, an heir apparent to Jordan, and in many ways, Oden/Durant is the mirror image of Bowie/Jordan.

Drafts are funny things. The '84 draft was in fact loaded with talent beyond the top three picks, but it's forever become known for the three major players — Olajuwon, Bowie, Jordan. But future Hall of Famers like Charles Barkley (the fifth overall pick) and John Stockton (selected 16th!) get easily forgotten under the shadow of Jordan and company. Even Sam Perkins and Kevin Willis had long, serviceable NBA careers, providing more ammunition in the argument for deepest draft on record. But the latter two have become footnotes in history. Booms and busts are what make a draft memorable — 1984 just happened to have both.

THE KIDS ARE ALL RIGHT, SOMETIMES

Ask fans to name the 13th pick overall in 1996 and they might be hard-pressed to come up with the name Kobe Bryant. Or two picks later, if you were to ask who was drafted 15th overall, would they be able to recall the greatest Canadian import in the history of the NBA, Steve Nash? That same draft was littered with future stars — Allen Iverson first overall, guards Peja Stoja-kovic (14th) and Derek Fisher (24th), and centers Jermaine O'Neal (17th) and Zydrunas Ilgauskas (20th). Although '84 may possess a plethora of Hall of Famers and an enticing story, '96 counts itself as one of the greatest drafts simply for the sheer number of men who went on to long, potent careers — and three future MVPs.

Bowie actually posted decent numbers his rookie season in the NBA — 10 points per game, 8.6 rebounds — but another broken leg the following year began a long streak of tibial fractures, this time to his right leg, derailing his once promising career, and the "bust" talk began in earnest. At the same time, Jordan was taking off, en route to championship after championship, dropping 40-plus with regularity while Bowie sat on the sidelines helplessly for more than two years. (Jordan, famously competitive, took distinct pleasure in torching Portland over the years for passing him over.) Bowie finally retired in 1995, averaging 10.9 points per game, 7.5 boards and nearly 2 blocks per contest over his career, not horrible numbers by any means, but for the man drafted before Jordan, for the man who played on two broken legs, those numbers will never be good enough.

Was it something in the water that year? Why do certain draft classes produce an inordinate number of NBA-ready stars? Basketball players enter the league at different points in their high school or college careers and enter the draft at various stages in their development. Some commit to four-year college programs and enter the NBA at 21 years of age, while others, like LeBron James — a man by the time he was able to drive — skip postsecondary

Philadelphia's Allen Iverson drives past a trio of Toronto Raptors, including rookie Chris Bosh (left), in 2003.

months of the year, and being older/faster/stronger at 12 or 13 is an advantage that allows those children to excel through the higher levels of the system.)

The 1996 draft class has been called one of the best of all time, with Bryant, Nash and Iverson all going on to win the MVP award — that's by far the most successful group of individuals out of any class. Future stars such as Stephon Marbury and Ray Allen went fourth and fifth, respectively. One can't help but think what the fate of the two Canadian expansion franchises, Toronto and Vancouver, might have been had they not chosen Marcus Camby and Shareef Abdur-Rahim at two and three in '96. Can you imagine being one of the GMs who passed on Bryant, Nash, Allen and Marbury? Camby and Abdur-Rahim turned out to be serviceable NBA players, but certainly not MVPs or All-Stars.

A legit number one can change a city. The aforementioned Iverson took Philly from joke squad to legit contender, making the NBA Finals in 2001. Kobe, however, became part of Phil Jackson's next big thing. His long-term consistency would have made any team better, but perhaps the hardest thing to gauge beyond talent is whether an 18- or 19-year-old has the mental fortitude, stamina and leadership skills to keep winning at a high level. For all the Bryants out of high school, there is a Jonathan Bender (fifth overall, Toronto, 1999), Darius Miles (third overall, LA Clippers, 2000) and DeSagana Diop (eighth overall, Cleveland, 2001) — all of them massive mistakes that have haunted those GMs for years.

For all the research, talent assessment, scouting and hand-wringing that go into drafting, how do so many teams get it wrong? Is it really just luck of the draw? This is what New Jersey Nets coach John Calipari (now head coach of Kentucky) said on draft night in 1996: "We really like Kobe. I think he's gonna be a terrific player in the NBA. But for us, right now, where we are and what we needed, I think in the end, [the right choice] was Kerry Kittles."

His is a common refrain: despite obviously talented players, teams often draft on need, not talent (or at least they used to). The Nets needed a forward that year, not a guard, similar to the Blazers in '84.

schooling altogether and enter the league at just 18. (This ended after the 2005 draft, when the league mandated that a player must turn 19 no later than December 31 of the year of the draft and be at least one year removed from high school graduation.)

A common refrain nowadays is "one-and-dones," players who possess the physical talent to play in the NBA at just 19 years of age and suit up for just one year of college. The 2014 first overall pick — and subsequent 2015 Rookie of the Year — Andrew Wiggins, did just that. He played one year at Kansas, a school dedicated to shaping one-and-dones, before abdicating to the NBA. If not for the rule change, he may have been a high school declarant.

There's no magic potion for why '96 or '84 exists, no Malcolm Gladwell moment to fall back on. (Gladwell argues that for hockey players, month of birth determines future success for NHLers because at certain age levels, kids are grouped together by birth month, and an inordinate number of NHL players are born in the first six

Carmelo Anthony, left, Dwyane Wade, center, and Chris Bosh make a media appearance prior to the 2003 NBA Draft. The trio were respectively selected third, fifth and fourth.

In 1996, Philadelphia 76ers GM Brad Greenberg, who had the first overall pick, said at the time that he didn't want a teenager. "I wasn't comfortable going with a [high school] kid for the number one pick vs. Iverson." In hindsight, despite Iverson's brilliance, he chose wrong when you consider the longevity of Bryant's career and what he meant to the Lakers. Iverson ended up doing wonders revitalizing the Philly basketball market, but he flamed out before winning anything substantial. Bryant went on to five rings. In the end, the 76ers missed out on a once-in-a-generation talent and a future Hall of Famer, but would they have done it differently?

It's important to remember that drafting an 18-year-old out of high school in the mid-90s was less common and ultimately seen as a gamble. When Minnesota took a teenaged Kevin Garnett fifth overall in 1995, it was seen as backwards thinking rather than as trendsetting.

Garnett proved his naysayers wrong and went on to have a spectacular career, but one without a championship for Minnesota. Yet he paved the way for Dwight Howard, LeBron and other high schoolers who made the jump to the Association.

FAST-FORWARD TO 2003 — a draft that rivals '96 and '84 in talent level. The draft had an immediate short-term talent impact on the NBA as well as a long-term one that would change the course of the NBA landscape, specifically in how teams are built and how teams win championships. Number one that year was a gimme. LeBron James was as automatic as they come, the greatest high schooler ever, a football player's build in a basketball player's body, and the hope was he would be a franchise changer for his hometown of Cleveland. Next pick — the only misstep of the top five — was Darko Milicic. The following three — Carmelo Anthony, Chris Bosh and Dwyane

Wade — became Olympians and All-Stars, and for Bosh, Wade and James, future champions with the Miami Heat twice over. It's the best top five ever seen, even inclusive of Milicic, and surely better than Jordan's draft year.

But more important is what happened later in their careers. When James and Bosh both opted out of their contracts to join Wade in 2010, a new era began in the NBA, one where players were suddenly mindful of taking control of their own destiny in a salary cap era. It was the ultimate recognition that no one individual can win a ring. James applied the same approach to team building when he rejoined the Cavaliers in 2014, opting out of his contract in Miami to sign with Cleveland. He was instrumental in convincing the brass to trade their number one pick, Canadian Andrew Wiggins, for Kevin Love. Along with point guard Kyrie Irving, the new trio formed a formidable threat and, in 2015–16, delivered the first championship to fans in Ohio in over 50 years.

GAMBLING IN THE LOTTERY ERA

For the first 20 years of the NBA Draft, beginning in 1964, a coin flip decided where a first pick landed. That flip could determine how a franchise might flourish or perish. Heads or tails. Pure luck. A 50/50 chance. But finally, in 1984, the NBA Board of Governors voted to introduce the lottery, a weighted system that gave the worst team in the NBA the greatest chance of securing the number one pick. The league has never looked back, and never has the marriage between ping-pong and basketball been so important to sport.

Fourteen numbered balls — one to fourteen — are stuffed in a drum. One thousand and one combinations exist, and each team in the lottery is assigned a four-number combo. To determine the draft order, four numbers are sucked up through the pipes. Whatever team has that combination wins the pick. The balls are returned, the process is repeated, and since then, the commissioner's familiar refrain can be heard through the rafters of the host city every June. "With the first pick in the NBA Draft, the [LUCKY TEAM NAME] selects . . ."

But beyond the obvious number ones that have emerged over the years, GMs are shifting away from drafting positionally and focusing on talent, especially overseas. Draft picks are inherently calculated gambles — small point guard and two-time MVP Steph Curry was taken seventh overall by Golden State — but sometimes they are just total freakin' long shots. Take Bruno Caboclo, the Toronto Raptors' 20th pick in 2014. Few had heard of him outside of a handful of NBA scouts and general managers. Projected to go second round, his selection was immediately questioned on social media. Who was this guy? Why would the Raptors blow their first-rounder on such an obscure kid? But GM Masai Ujiri saw something in Caboclo. Long on potential — he has an enormous 7-foot-6 wingspan — the raw rookie represents exactly the type of risk teams are willing to make in a growing international market. Teams aren't focused on drafting a big man like they were in the 80s with Bowie. Size, speed, long arms for defense and a predilection for hitting a three are all more important than a big body in the middle. And with the success of the Spurs — drafting an unknown commodity such as Tony Parker from Europe — teams are more comfortable taking risks with international players, particularly if it doesn't cost them salary while they hone their skills in European basketball leagues. Additionally, there's more parity in talent level than ever before.

Current Cleveland Cavaliers GM David Griffin said at the 2014

draft: "I don't think there's a clear cut number one pick in most drafts. I think when people say that, they have a really strong feeling for one player over another, but there's not necessarily a consensus." The same might be said for lower picks like Caboclo. Ujiri, perhaps worried another general manager would snap up his guy before the second round, weighed the risk and deemed it acceptable. He and the Raptors can now develop the player as they see fit. The reality is most picks don't pan out anyway, and it's likely Caboclo may not be a productive NBA player — as of 2017, he was still a reserve on the team and played most of his minutes in the D-League. But if he becomes productive . . . boom. Smartest thing the Raptors ever did.

BOOMS AND BUSTS. That's what sticks in the minds of many as they look back on the greatest drafts in the history of the league. For every Michael Jordan, there's a Sam Bowie. Taken before the greatest basketball player to ever live, Bowie became an unfortunate punch line, a player who could never live up to expectations. Perhaps history has been unkind to him. Or maybe for every Jordan, there are a thousand Sam Bowies, a thousand hopefuls who dream of NBA stardom. The hope and the dream of every NBA executive is choosing the right one.

KYRIE IRVING

SAN ANTONIO SPURS

POSITION POWER FORWARD–CENTER / **SHOOTS** RIGHT / **HEIGHT** 6'11" / **WEIGHT** 260 LB. / **DRAFTED** 2006, CHICAGO BULLS, 2ND OVERALL

LAMARCUS ALDRIDGE 12

LAMARCUS ALDRIDGE PREVIOUSLY carried the Portland Trail Blazers on his broad shoulders for nine seasons, saving his best for the 2014–15 campaign. But entering his prime years, the 6-foot-11 center elected to join the San Antonio Spurs as a free agent and now carries the mantle of recently retired legend Tim Duncan. With San Antonio's aging duo of Tony Parker and Manu Ginobili coming back for another try at a championship, Aldridge will be a key cog in extending the legacy of the Spurs.

Born July 19, 1985, in Dallas, Aldridge was a longtime work in progress. Before starring at the University of Texas for two years and leapfrogging to the NBA, he was a skinny 6-foot-7 eighth grader with a limited arsenal and a weak hook shot. But a similarly sized older brother and an inspirational coach coaxed Aldridge to improve and not be discouraged. By his senior year in high school the lessons and hard work paid off, and he averaged 30 points and 14 rebounds per game. Once at Texas, Aldridge helped his alma mater reach the Elite Eight. His coach there said he'd "never had a player work harder to get better."

Selected second overall in the 2006 draft by the Chicago Bulls, Aldridge was instantly traded to Portland, becoming the fulcrum of a Trail Blazers team in search of a new identity after a long stretch missing the playoffs. In Portland he was able to showcase all of his many talents. His

midrange jumper for a nearly seven-footer is almost unbeatable, and he's ruthlessly efficient from the normally difficult-to-hit-from distance. Alongside tenacious point guard Damian Lillard, another emerging

star in the NBA, the duo formed a one-two tandem that was one of the best in the league. Aldridge has been praised for a strong basketball IQ and his commitment to hard work and fitness. The latter has

helped him rebound from early career adversity that saw him contend with numerous niggling injuries and the diagnosis of a heart condition that required him to take considerable time away from the court. But the work he put in has allowed him to find the top of his game.

During one game in the 2013–14 season, Aldridge hauled down 25 boards to go along with 31 points, a phenomenal display that set a career best in rebounds. In the 2014 playoffs, he showed just how far he'd come, putting up dominant numbers in the first two games of Portland's series against the Houston Rockets, and on the road to boot. His first was a statement 46-point and 18-rebound game. It matched his career high for points in any contest and eclipsed his own previous playoff scoring record while also demolishing Portland's franchise mark. "I want to try and break every record I can," he said following the game.

In 2014–15, his last season in Portland, he finished eighth in the league in defensive rebounds and 10th in total rebounds per game (all despite injuring his thumb in late January). Rather than elect to undergo surgery for the injury, Aldridge played through the pain, a testament to his toughness

and how much he wants to win. His 23.4 points per game in 2014–15 set a career high. And following the thumb injury? He went back-to-back with 37 and 38 points versus top Eastern Conference foes Cleveland and Atlanta, adding 11 boards in each game and even dropping a pair of threes in each contest.

In his first season in San Antonio, Aldridge barely missed a beat while playing alongside legendary Spurs center Tim Duncan. Highlights from the season included a 36-point night versus the New Orleans Pelicans and a Western Conference Player of the Week honor in February 2016. The Spurs finished with a home record of 40-1, tying a record set by Larry Bird and the Celtics in 1985–86, but were ousted in the playoffs by Oklahoma despite Aldridge's racking up two huge games — 38 points and 42 points in the first two games, respectively. Aldridge finished the regular season with 18.3 points and 8.5 rebounds over 74 games as he adjusted to a new role in San Antonio.

His numbers in 2016–17 were ruthlessly consistent, averaging over 17 points and 7 boards per game. The Spurs returned to the Western Conference finals under Aldridge's

- Named an NBA All-Rookie (First Team) in 2006–07
- Has played in five All-Star Games (2012–2016)
- Was an All-NBA Second Team selection for 2014–15
- Set a career high in points (46) in 2013–14
- Is a nine-time NBA Player of the Week

watch but were swept by the Golden State Warriors. He's signed with the franchise until 2019.

The five-time All-Star has established himself as one of the most unstoppable forwards in the game, a threat from anywhere on the court. His foot speed and ball skills are a nightmare for a man who matches him in size, and his 89-inch wingspan is an absolute disaster of a matchup for an undersized player. Having brought his talents to Texas, the Spurs got a player that fits their system perfectly. He can pass the ball and he is terrific in the post — musts for San Antonio bigs. With Aldridge in the fold, don't be surprised to see the Black and Silver vying for another title.

POSITION SHOOTING GUARD / **SHOOTS** RIGHT / **HEIGHT** 6'7" / **WEIGHT** 231 LB. / **DRAFTED** 2011, CHICAGO BULLS, 30TH OVERALL

JIMMY BUTLER 21

AT 6-FOOT-7 AND 231 pounds, with guard skills and big size, Jimmy Butler is part of an emerging class of NBA stars who can play multiple roles and who bring a different, exciting blend of athleticism to the NBA. Between 2011–12 and 2016–17 Butler became the face of the Chicago Bulls with the departure of Pau Gasol, Joakim Noah and Derrick Rose. And after veteran Dwyane Wade mentored the shooting guard in 2016–17, Butler now seems braced to take the leap to superstardom.

Butler's backstory is one of perseverance and overcoming a stacked deck. With his family life in disarray outside Houston, Texas, it's a wonder he was able to make it. Abandoned by his father at birth and kicked out of the house by his mother at 13, Butler could have easily slipped through the cracks. But he ultimately persevered, living with a friend's family in the outskirts of Houston in a town called Tomball. With talent that was off the charts and an incredible drive to learn, Butler averaged nearly 20 points and 9 rebounds a game during his senior year of high school. In 2017, Tomball High raised his No. 1 jersey to the rafters.

Butler was a slow but steady worker — he was ranked just 73rd in the entire state of Texas before jumping from high school to junior college ball. He excelled and moved up to NCAA Division I school Marquette University after Marquette's coach noticed him while scouting another player at Butler's junior college. He played three years at Marquette, averaging 15.7 points in his final season under coach Buzz Williams, a tough-nosed drill sergeant whom Butler credits for instilling in him a tenacious work ethic and never-stop attitude. But even when Butler's stock rose after his promising stint at Marquette, he still was unheralded coming out of college, taken 30th overall by Chicago in the 2011 draft.

In January 2013 he made a big impression on Bulls teammates and fans alike after his strong defense held the legendary Kobe Bryant to just 7 of 22 from the field, acquiring the nickname "Kobe Stopper" as he strutted off the court. Butler continued impressing his colleagues on the defensive end, facing up against LeBron James in the playoffs and cementing a rep as one of the few men in the league who can limit King James' numbers. In early 2014 Butler played 60 minutes in a triple OT thriller versus the Orlando Magic, the most minutes in Bulls history and tied for eighth most of all time; he can thank his college coach for all those wind sprints.

Butler's a three-time NBA All-Star, he won the 2015 award for most improved player, and he scored a gold medal playing on the 2016 U.S. men's Olympic basketball team, an experience that launched him into the discussion about the best young players in the game.

In 2016–17 Butler easily eclipsed his 2015–16 points total, finishing the season with 23.9 points per game and becoming the go-to guy in the Bulls' offensive scheme. He put the first punctuation mark on the power transfer just after Christmas when he hit the game-winning shot versus the Brooklyn Nets to finish with 40 on the night. The play the coach drew up? "Give the ball to Jimmy." It was a game in which Wade left with a migraine and Butler took over. It wouldn't be the last time. He scorched the Charlotte Hornets for 53 points in early January 2017 and dropped two clutch late-game free throws for a win versus the Boston Celtics right before the All-Star break. He registered his first triple-double of the season against a

LeBron-less Cleveland Cavaliers team in late February, posting a line of 18 points, 10 boards and 10 helpers. Plus, he's a minute-muncher, cruising over 36 minutes per contest.

In June 2017 Butler was traded to the Minnesota Timberwolves in a deal that saw Zach LaVine, Kris Dunn and 7th overall pick Lauri Markkanen move into the Bulls' locker room. With Butler on their team, the promising young T-Wolves will undoubtedly be the squad to watch in the coming seasons.

CAREER HIGHLIGHTS

- Named NBA Most Improved Player for 2014–15
- Named to NBA All-Defensive Second Team three times (2013–14, 2014–15, 2015–16)
- Has played in three All-Star Games (2015–2017)
- Named Eastern Conference Player of the Week for January 2017
- Won an Olympic gold medal with the U.S. men's basketball team in Rio 2016

POSITION POINT GUARD / **SHOOTS** LEFT / **HEIGHT** 6'1" / **WEIGHT** 175 LB. / **DRAFTED** 2007, MEMPHIS GRIZZLIES, 4TH OVERALL

MIKE CONLEY 11

AT 6-FOOT-1 AND 175 pounds, Mike Conley isn't the biggest point guard in the league. And despite his name being absent from conversations about the best players at the position, he's quickly become the fulcrum of a resurgent Memphis Grizzlies team that's challenging for league supremacy. Make no mistake: Mike Conley has slowly matured into one of the most consistent difference makers in the NBA today.

Conley comes from athletic pedigree — his father, Mike Conley Sr., won gold at the 1992 Olympics in triple jump, and his uncle played linebacker for the Pittsburgh Steelers. Mike starred at Ohio State as a point guard for one season for the Buckcycs alongside future number one pick Greg Oden. The duo led the school to the 2007 NCAA final, where they lost to a powerhouse Florida team. Conley was

drafted fourth overall by the Memphis Grizzlies in 2007. But before making the jump to Ohio and then the NBA, Oden and Conley were a force to be reckoned with, destroying the high school basketball scene in Indiana while amassing a 103-7 record with Lawrence North High School in Indianapolis. The duo led the Hoosier state to three state championships.

When Ohio State coach Thad Matta recruited the two stars together, he said that at the time people laughed at him because he thought Conley was "the best point guard in the country," despite the fact that "he played with Greg." Matta, of course, is having the last laugh now (though not so much for Oden, who was hampered by injuries and never amounted to the hype).

Conley, on the other hand, has been durable and effective, running the offense for the Grizz over the last 10 years. In 2016–17 he posted a career-high 20.5 points per game in addition to 6.3 assists. The court general has maintained a free-throw percentage of more than 80 percent and has shot 37.9 percent from behind the arc his entire NBA career. He may not lead the Grizzlies in any one category, but his presence on the court and what he means to his team aren't found on the score sheet. One of his first coaches in the league, Johnny Davis, commented in early 2015 that Conley was "as important to the success of the Grizzlies as Zach Randolph and

which is the farthest the franchise has gone in its history.

The 2014–15 playoffs were tough on the undersized guard. Already playing with a wonky ankle, he suffered a facial fracture that required surgery at the end of the Grizzlies' first-round victory over the Portland Trail Blazers. Conley gamely came back in the second round wearing a face mask versus the Golden State Warriors and sparked the Grizz to victory in Game 2 on the road — the Warriors' first loss in Oakland in 22 games dating back to the regular season. Conley's 22 points on 8-of-10 shooting underscore the emotional impact he brought to the arena that night, but it wasn't enough, and the Grizzlies' season ended at the hands of Golden State. In 2016–17, after re-signing with Memphis for a then-league-high $153 million over five years, Conley didn't simply sit on his newfound dough — he averaged a career best in points (20.5) and rebounds (3.5) per game and hit treys at a 40 percent clip. There were several nights throughout the season when he hit at least seven from behind the arc.

Conley's been labeled both an underachiever and underrated, but it's about time both tags are shed in favor of what he actually is: the key cog in the offense of one of the most consistent teams in the NBA — and one of the NBA's brightest stars.

Marc Gasol. He has evolved into one of the better point guards in the league."

It's been slow and steady progress, however. He started just 46 games his rookie year. By year two, he clocked in at 60, but his numbers were average (10.9 points per game, 4.3 assists — hardly bulletin board material for the fourth overall pick), and he was sharing time in an untenable situation with future All-Star Kyle Lowry, who'd been drafted one year ahead of Conley. Lowry was eventually traded in 2009 to Houston, and Conley took over the Grizzlies' point guard position for good.

He plays primarily left-handed — despite actually being right-handed — but uses his right to drain his money shot, a short-range floater that he's been good for at more than 50 percent in recent years.

Perhaps his most admirable, unquantifiable quality is his ability to get guys going. Conley is a whiz at noticing when his teammates need the ball — "it's almost like you have a clock in your head," he once said — or knowing when he needs to slash toward the hoop to give the team an energy boost. He helped take the team to the Western Conference finals in 2012,

DEMARCUS COUSINS [0]

WHEN YOU'RE 6-FOOT-6 in eighth grade, certain things seem likely. For instance, if you have a single athletic bone in your body, and you don't mind hitting people, chances are you'll find yourself on a football field. That is exactly where DeMarcus Cousins found himself as a youth. Just as likely was that Cousins would be a shoo-in to rule the basketball court. Yet, at 14 he'd never really played. Destiny, however, has a way of carving a path. After a chance encounter with an AAU recruiter, who thought the eighth grader was a high school senior, Cousins got his basketball start. The following year, he dominated older, bigger boys as a high school freshman, averaging 26 points, 15 rebounds and 10 assists per game with a ridiculous .700 shooting percentage. His one season of stellar play landed him on the national radar.

Born in Mobile, Alabama, Cousins flourished on the hardwood, dazzling scouts with the hands of a guard and the size of a forward. But despite a gregarious, engaging personality outside of the gym, Cousins was plagued by a reputation as a hothead on the court. He carried the stigma into college, no thanks to a suspension during high school for shoving a teacher after an argument.

Cousins spent just one year at Kentucky before jumping to the Association. A fan favorite there despite playing just over 20 minutes per game, he still managed 15 points and 10 rebounds per contest. His coach, John Calipari, said Cousins was "one of the most talented big men I've ever had." Calipari went on to cite Cousins' ball-handling skills and his "mean streak" as positives for the prospect.

Before the 2010 NBA Draft — where Cousins would go fifth overall to Sacramento — the center played 1-on-1 with Kevin Durant, and despite getting crossed up, he returned the favor to the former MVP, which did not go unnoticed by the Oklahoma City star. In his rookie year Cousins turned heads with his skill set, and he put up respectable numbers: 14.1 points per game and 8.6 rebounds. The following year, despite turmoil with then-Kings coach Paul

- Named an NBA All-Rookie (First Team) in 2010–11
- Has played in three All-Star Games (2015–17)
- Led the NBA in offensive rebounds (265) in 2011–12
- Led the NBA in defensive rebound percentage (30.5) in 2013–14
- Has finished in the top 10 for six consecutive years in rebounds per game (2011–12 to 2016–17)

Westphal, Cousins' stats improved in all facets, including steals and blocks. But he wasn't living up to his potential, and the Kings continued to be awful. (Their last winning season was 2005–06.)

At 6-foot-11 and 270 pounds, "Boogie" is one of the best bigs in the NBA. Case in point: in the third game of the 2014–15 season, he put up 34 points and 18 rebounds against Blake Griffin and the LA Clippers, a statement game considering Griffin won Rookie of the Year in Cousins' inaugural campaign. In 2015–16, Cousins had a night to remember, scoring 56 points in a double OT loss to the Charlotte Hornets. He hit 21 of 30 from the field and hauled down 12 boards in one of the top individual efforts of the season from any NBA player. It was a tantalizing display of the potential the center possesses.

Cousins' success isn't without its problems. His career has been marred by his temper and technical fouls. In 2012–13, he led the NBA with 17 Ts and tied with Griffin and Durant for the league lead the following season. In 2014–15 he couldn't stay true to his preseason promise of five Ts or fewer, and by season's end he was once again one of the NBA's worst aggressors, racking up 14 Ts for third most in the league. In 2015–16 and 2016–17 he followed along the same lines, finishing the seasons with 17 and 18 technical fouls, respectively. But maybe Cousins' foul trouble isn't that big a

deal. People don't waste a lot of breath talking about Russell Westbrook's penchant for getting T'd up. He led the NBA in 2014–15 and has been one of the league's worst offenders. (Westbrook finished second behind Cousins in 2016-17.) The lack of emphasis on Westbrook's foul trouble seems a double standard — and perhaps linked more to Cousins' position and reputation than anything else.

Despite his best offensive season to date in 2016–17 — he finished seventh in scoring — Cousins was traded by Sacramento at

the conclusion of the 2017 All-Star Game to the New Orleans Pelicans, a move that caught everyone off guard, including the center. He finished the year in Louisiana, averaging 27 points and 11 rebounds.

Cousins is barely on the precipice of his prime, so the sky's the limit for his individual success. Will a change of zip code alter the course of his career? Can he and Anthony Davis form the most formidable front court in the NBA? One thing is certain: whatever team Cousins plays for is better off with him than without.

POSITION SHOOTING GUARD / **SHOOTS** RIGHT / **HEIGHT** 6'7" / **WEIGHT** 220 LB. / **DRAFTED** 2009, TORONTO RAPTORS, 9TH OVERALL

DEMAR DEROZAN 10

IT'S BEEN HARD to label DeMar DeRozan a superstar quite yet, difficult to mention him in the company of NBA greats. But slowly, surely, quietly and diligently, the face of the Toronto Raptors has been putting in work, and it's finally paying off for the shooting guard, both in career numbers and team success for the Raptors.

Even at 6-foot-7, DeRozan's athletic frame appears more compact and lean than oversized. The product of Compton High School and USC, DeRozan has always surprised pundits with his smooth dribbling, sweet jumper and knack for getting to the line. But make no mistake, he's always been lethal, and as a high school freshman he averaged 26.1 points and 8.4 rebounds. He was so gifted that not only could he dunk at 12 years old, but even the gang members in his neighborhood chose not to mess with the family of the talented young man who stayed loyal to his hometown high school rather than jumping ship for a more prestigious place to play.

Forgoing the final three years of his NCAA eligibility after one season at USC, where he was named Pac-10 tournament MVP, the athletic guard was selected by the Toronto Raptors ninth overall in 2009. While other players have shunned playing in Canada or elected to move elsewhere to pursue better opportunities to win after their entry-level contracts were complete, DeRozan has stepped up. Toronto was where he wanted to be, and despite several losing seasons to begin his tenure, the last few years have paid dividends, and DeRozan's emerged as a leader and the go-to guy on the team.

His size on the defensive end against smaller guards is difficult to get past, and he can guard undersized forwards on the wing, a versatility hard to find in the NBA.

his first lengthy layoff after tearing an adductor muscle, which forced him out for 21 games. And although it took some time to find his form, DeRozan propped up the Raptors while the team battled injuries and inconsistent play. In March 2015, DeRozan dropped a cool 35 on the Philadelphia 76ers and then followed that up with 25 against Cleveland. He has become the guy the Raptors want taking shots late in the game, staring down opponents and going 1-on-1 with the shot clock winding down. A quiet confidence oozes from his eyes, a steely look that means business, the look of a cold-blooded killer ready to do it again. You see it in the eyes of the NBA's best, and the Raptors guard is forcing commentators to include him in that category as his career stretches on. He has made the playoffs four consecutive years, including a 2016 run into the conference finals.

If there's one knock against the pro, it's his three-point shooting, which has climbed only twice above the 30 percent mark. But there's no need to add that to his arsenal yet — he's still slashing and driving, turning around defenders with a crossover and draining difficult turnaround Js. And all that pressure helps him make it to the line. By far, the 2016–17 season will go down as DeRozan's finest to date. He finished fifth in NBA scoring, averaging over 27 points per game, and touched the 40-point mark seven times. With Kyle Lowry injured, DeRozan single-handedly dominated opponents late in the season, including a Herculean 43 against division rivals the Boston Celtics. The 2017 playoffs ended in disappointment; after scraping past the Milwaukee Bucks in the first round, the Toronto Raptors fell to LeBron James and the Cleveland Cavaliers for the second straight year.

If he hasn't come into his own already, DeRozan's about to stand at the peak and look off into the distance because he's finally risen to the top of the mountain. With a fourth straight playoff berth, a bright future looms in Toronto. And it all hinges on the boy from Compton who decided to call Canada his second home.

CAREER HIGHLIGHTS

- Has played in three All-Star Games (2014, 2016, 2017)
- Named Eastern Conference Player of the Month for April 2015 and January 2016
- Was a four-time NBA Player of the Week in 2016–17
- Drafted by the Toronto Raptors in the first round (9th overall) in 2009
- Won an Olympic gold medal with the U.S. men's basketball team in Rio in 2016

From the line, DeRozan is equally dangerous, averaging over 80 percent from the stripe and making teams pay for hacking at his arms as he nimbly darts to the hoop. He put up then-career numbers in 2013–14 as he led the Raptors to the playoffs for the first time in five years. His 22.7 points per game went along with 4.3 boards and 4 assists, and he was top 10 in the league in getting to the line, where he shot 82.4 percent.

Over the past eight seasons, DeRozan has been a horse, logging nearly 35 minutes per contest. In 2014–15, however, he faced

POSITION SMALL FORWARD / **SHOOTS** RIGHT / **HEIGHT** 6'9" / **WEIGHT** 220 LB. / **DRAFTED** 2010, INDIANA PACERS, 10TH OVERALL

PAUL GEORGE 13

IT WAS ONE of the freakiest injuries anyone in basketball had ever seen. In a scrimmage to decide the U.S. roster for the 2014 FIBA World Cup, Paul George suffered a gruesome broken leg when he slammed into the backboard stanchion trying to block a James Harden shot in transition defense. The injury kept him off the court for most of the 2014–15 season, and many questioned whether the forward would ever be the same player. He put the criticism to rest with a miraculous season in 2015–16, reestablishing his status among the NBA elite and leading the Indiana Pacers back to the playoffs. But there's still work to do for the star as he sails into his prime.

At 6-foot-9 and 220 pounds, George is tall, athletic and in possession of a shot that's nearly impossible to stop even when a smaller opponent is draped all over him. That's the problem. It doesn't matter if you match up a bigger man against George — he's too smooth. If you go small, he'll use his body to get the defender out of the way. He had his strongest season following that devastating injury, averaging 23.1 points per contest to go along with 7 boards and 4.1 assists — a testament to his recovery efforts. He provided the fuel needed by the Pacers engine, recording four 40-point games that season, one a 48-point effort versus the Utah Jazz on 15-of-27 shooting, including 8 three-pointers.

Drafted 10th overall in 2010, George spent two years playing college ball at Fresno State in California, near his hometown of Palmdale. He wasn't as highly touted in the state of California as DeMar DeRozan, but he was a player to watch. George averaged 16.3 points in his second and final year of college before making the jump to the NBA. His draft class was loaded with talent — John Wall and DeMarcus Cousins went first and fifth, respectively, and Utah picked Gordon Hayward just before George. Arguably, the Pacers picked the best small forward available.

He was a one-man difference maker in the first-round playoff matchup versus the Toronto Raptors in 2015–16, stuffing DeRozan on defense with his length and

providing nearly all the Pacers' offense in the seven-game-series loss. He was easily the best player in the series and proved he has the cojones to keep up in a tough playoff matchup.

The next season was an interesting story. He concluded 2016 with back-to-back 30-plus-point efforts, and the product of Fresno State began consistently putting up big numbers in 2017. He was an All-Star once again (his fourth time), but George didn't have the type of breakout season Indiana fans were hoping for, even though he single-handedly willed the Pacers into the 2017 playoffs. Despite George's strong play at both ends of the floor guarding LeBron James during the first round, the Pacers were swept by the Cleveland Cavaliers.

In a league where James Harden and Russell Westbrook are triple-double vending machines, George is still middle of the pack when it comes to points from superstars. At the All-Star break he hadn't cracked the top 20 in points, although his free-throw shooting was top five in the league that season. The bottom line is he'll need to pick it up in at least one of the three top categories if he wants to soar to a new stratosphere.

George has received a few key accolades — he was named the league's most improved player in 2013 and won gold with the U.S. men's Olympic squad in 2016. But he's got his eyes set on a different prize — one in the form of a championship ring.

In June 2017, just before the free-agent deadline, the Pacers traded George to

Oklahoma City for Victor Oladipo and Domantas Sabonis. This league-rocking deal potentially gives Russell Westbrook and the Thunder squad the ammunition they need to rise to the top of the dominant west and George a very real shot at a championship.

CAREER HIGHLIGHTS

- Named NBA Most Improved Player for 2012–13
- Named to NBA All-Defensive First Team in 2013–14
- Has played in four All-Star Games (2013–14, 2016–17)
- Named Eastern Conference Player of the Month for April 2017
- Won an Olympic gold medal with the U.S. men's basketball team in Rio in 2016

POSITION POWER FORWARD / **SHOOTS** RIGHT / **HEIGHT** 6'10" / **WEIGHT** 251 LB. / **DRAFTED** 2009, LOS ANGELES CLIPPERS, 1ST OVERALL

BLAKE GRIFFIN 32

BLAKE GRIFFIN LIKELY needs no introduction. You've probably seen him soaring through the air, high above the rim, waiting for a lob pass before slamming the ball into the bucket below. Griffin is more than just the meat and potatoes of the Los Angeles Clippers franchise — he's a multidimensional power forward who's quickly become one of the most versatile and exciting players in the NBA, a star since day one.

At 6-foot-10 and 251 pounds, it's hard to contend with his size. Griffin's a muscular, agile forward, with speed to the hoop and Superman-like ability to play above the rim. He was born in Oklahoma City and suited up for the Sooners in college. By his sophomore season, he'd emerged as the best player in the country; he declared for the draft after notching 22.7 points per game and 14.4 rebounds in his second year at Oklahoma.

Taken number one overall by the Clippers, Griffin's presence immediately changed the franchise — although it took an extra year for the transformation to happen on the floor, thanks to a preseason knee injury that kept him sidelined for all of 2009–10. By the time he finally threw on a Clips jersey, Griffin's star-like abilities were obvious. He twice topped 40 points in 2010–11, dropping 44 against New York early in the season and 47 versus Indiana later that campaign. He was a unanimous choice for Rookie of the Year, beating out future All-Star John Wall and becoming

the first rookie since Ralph Sampson in 1984 to sweep the award. He averaged 22.1 points, 12.1 boards and 3.8 assists. But it wasn't just that. Griffin managed two triple-doubles and amassed a miraculous 63 double-doubles for the third highest total in the league. He finished three shy of that year's leader, Dwight Howard, a staggering achievement for a rookie.

Griffin's spectacular first year had shades of another great's rookie campaign.

Shaquille O'Neal, the former LA Lakers and Orlando Magic star, posted 23.9 points and 13.9 rebounds his inaugural year in the league, and he added 3.5 blocks. Despite this, O'Neal was not a unanimous selection for best first-year player like Griffin. Upon receiving the award in 2011, Griffin said, "To miss my entire first year and then be able to be up here today is definitely satisfying." The Clippers, however, didn't make the playoffs, finishing 32-50. The

havoc. Despite a slight dip in his numbers, Griffin still led the team with averages of 18 points and 8.7 boards, while Paul dished out 9.7 dimes per game. The team finished 56-26 but fell to the Memphis Grizzlies in the first round, a disappointing exit for a strong team.

In 2014–15 the Clippers' longtime center DeAndre Jordan had a career year (he posted the second highest field goal percentage in NBA history), and despite an up-and-down season for the Clips that saw them score the second most points per game in the league while giving up the 16th most — all while still dealing with the fallout of Donald Sterling's racist comments — the team still finished 56-26. Griffin suffered an elbow injury in early 2015 that kept him out of the lineup for 15 games, but he came back strong, torching the Golden State Warriors for 40 points and 12 rebounds in just his ninth game back.

Although his numbers have been slightly down the past three seasons — perhaps due to Jordan's emergence up the middle and injuries that have kept Griffin sidelined for long periods of time — Griffin has added to his game, unleashing a step-back jumper that's nearly automatic when he's left open. It used to be that Griffin would almost always take the ball to the hoop. Now defenders need to do a little guesswork.

But 2016–17 ended with another disappointing first-round playoff exit, one in which Griffin injured his foot and needed surgery. For long-starved Clippers fans desperate for a title and bragging rights in a crowded California market, Griffin's been a key component in the team's reaching the postseason six straight seasons, and with career numbers of 21 points and 8.5 rebounds per game, he's almost irreplaceable. But entering a contract year in 2018 and with Paul now lobbing for the Houston Rockets, Griffin will have to decide if he wants to keep leaping for LA or take his talents elsewhere in the second half of his career.

team's fortunes would change when they traded for Chris Paul later that year.

The pair immediately became the core of Lob City, a high-flying, acrobatic group that was a threat from the air every time they ran the ball upcourt during the lockout-shortened season of 2011–12. The Clips finished 40-26 and made the postseason for the first time since 2006, ringing in a new era in Los Angeles despite a second-round loss to San Antonio. In their first full season together the following year, Paul and Griffin continued to wreak

POSITION POINT GUARD / **SHOOTS** RIGHT / **HEIGHT** 6'3" / **WEIGHT** 193 LB. / **DRAFTED** 2011, CLEVELAND CAVALIERS, 1ST OVERALL

KYRIE IRVING [2]

THE TALENT IS there. The personality is too. What Kyrie Irving needed to become one of the greatest stars in the NBA was to take the always elusive next step. And after the point guard dropped two 50-point games in 2014–15, it was the first sign he'd finally arrived. It was also the precursor to his game-winning shot in Game 7 of the 2016 NBA Finals that awarded the city of Cleveland its first professional sports championship in 52 years.

Irving's path to stardom isn't run of the mill. He was born in Melbourne, Australia, and raised in New Jersey. His father played professionally down under before relocating to the Garden State, where the younger Irving flourished. Irving owes a lot to his father, who failed to make the NBA but ensured his son would, stating boldly that Kyrie would be the best player in New Jersey. The positive thinking wore off: Irving, who was dribbling a ball at just 13 months old, wrote himself a note in fourth grade that said "GOAL: PLAY IN THE NBA."

First he went to Duke, where he played just 11 games his first season because of a toe injury. By then, even with the limited college trial, everyone knew the talented guard. In a classic case of one-and-done, Irving declared for the draft and was selected first overall by the Cleveland Cavaliers. In his rookie season he averaged 18.5 points per game, 5.4 assists and a shooting percentage of .469 en route to Rookie of the Year honors despite missing

15 games. But playing for a hapless Cavs team wasn't ideal for the rising star, and the team finished with a 21-45 record. His point-per-game totals increased the following season by a whopping 4 points, but the Cavs still failed to make waves in the Eastern Conference. Soon he'd not only be swimming with sharks, he was the shark. In the 2013–14 All-Star Game, Irving chucked up 31 points and dished out 14 assists on the way to being named MVP. That same season he posted the first triple-double of his career against the Utah Jazz with a line of 21 points, 12 assists and 10 rebounds. He was beginning to impress the league with his scoring punch and consistency, and he also garnered attention for his famous "Uncle Drew" character in Pepsi Max commercials.

However, Irving's career will probably be remembered in two distinct phases: pre-LeBron and post-LeBron. With the arrival in Cleveland of the four-time MVP to start the 2014–15 season, Irving hit the jackpot. His career averages saw only a slight uptick with James in the mix, but with the explosive forward gobbling up the majority of attention from defenders, Irving is being given time to shine in ways he hasn't before. He is the Cavs' driving force, the straw that stirs the drink. He is a shifty point guard with top-level dribbling skills capable of running the floor, dishing the rock or stepping back to hit a timely trey. Take the night that Irving, with LeBron nursing a wrist injury, stung the talent-heavy Portland Trail Blazers for 55 points in a 99–94 win. Irving sunk 11 three-pointers and went a perfect 10 for 10 from the stripe in what was then a career high for points. Not to be outdone by even himself, the point guard upped the ante and sent a message to the entire league with his 57-point performance against the reigning-champion San Antonio Spurs. "The kid is special," James said following the game. Charles Barkley called it "one of the best individual performances I've ever seen."

But it's not only LeBron who's made Cleveland a better squad since Irving's rookie season — the addition of Kevin

Love, Kyle Korver and Tristan Thompson makes this a talent-laden, veteran-heavy team and a perennial contender in the East. The 2014–15 season saw the Cavs make it all the way to Game 6 of the NBA Finals, despite a knee injury to Irving in Game 1. Irving averaged 19 points, 3.8 assists and 3.9 rebounds over 13 playoff games and was sorely missed as a three-point threat in the finals (he'd been shooting 45 percent). He'd avenge the loss the following season. Finally healthy midway through the year — he played just 53 regular-season games, averaging 19.6 points and 4.7 assists — Irving was primed for playoff basketball after dropping a cool 35 points in the second-to-last game of the season versus Atlanta, his season high. Irving saved his best for the NBA Finals, hitting the game-winning three-point dagger that toppled the Golden State Warriors in the final minute of Game 7. It's become Irving's signature highlight, delivering the Cavaliers their first NBA championship in franchise history.

In 2016–17 he was a horse, averaging 25

points per game, nearly 6 dimes, 90 percent from the stripe and 40 percent from beyond the arc. Season highlights include a triumphant 49-point game in late January against the New Orleans Pelicans — 35 of those scored in the second half alone.

It's an exciting time to be Irving. He weathered some lean years in Cleveland to begin his career, and now the team's a perennial threat in the Eastern Conference and an NBA champion. With a young, healthy Irving and a dominant, still-in-his-prime LeBron, Cleveland fans are hoping this recent NBA title is the first of many.

CAREER HIGHLIGHTS

- Named NBA Rookie of the Year for 2011–12
- Named the All-Star Game MVP in 2014
- Named an NBA All-Rookie (First Team) in 2011–12
- Was an All-NBA Third Team selection for 2014–15
- Has played in four All-Star Games (2013–2015, 2017)

POSITION POINT GUARD / **SHOOTS** RIGHT / **HEIGHT** 6'3" / **WEIGHT** 195 LB. / **DRAFTED** 2012, PORTLAND TRAIL BLAZERS, 6TH OVERALL

DAMIAN LILLARD⁰

DAMIAN LILLARD SHOULD need no introduction to anyone who has watched the Portland Trail Blazers play during the past five years. The point guard from Oakland has firmly established himself as the future of the franchise and one of the rising stars in the NBA.

The most impressive thing you can call a basketball player is clutch. And that's what Lillard proved himself to be in the 2014 playoffs, ending a long drought for Portland fans who'd been waiting to see their team travel beyond the first round. Some have called his game-winning basket in Game 6 versus the Houston Rockets the greatest shot in Trail Blazers history. Lillard's heroics cemented the first playoff series win in 14 years and endeared him to a fan base starving for a championship.

Nights like that will define Lillard's career for years to come. He grew up tough and quickly — you have to on the streets of Oakland. With that toughness came an obsession — he was always at the gym as a kid, looking for a game. His older brother once described him as "fearless." But Lillard was undersized and, in his own words in 2012, "overlooked." Few scholarship offers from big schools came his way, and he opted to attend Weber State in Utah, a mid-major that's not exactly on the national radar. But with a tenacity and scoring ability that saw him post 24.5 points, 5 rebounds and 4 assists per game, he was propelled to the top of the ranks by

his junior season, and he skipped senior year to head into the draft, where the Trail Blazers grabbed him with the sixth pick in 2012. It was a steal.

Slow to make a name for himself out of high school, he wasted no time as a professional, entering the NBA with a bang. Lillard put up 23 points and 11 assists in his debut and never looked back, torching the league in his rookie campaign. He finished with 19 points, 6.5 assists and 3.1 rebounds per game and was a unanimous decision for Rookie of the Year. Playing all 82 games for the second straight season in his sophomore campaign (2013–14), Lillard proved his inaugural season was no fluke, posting nearly identical numbers and increasing his threat to score from behind the arc to nearly 40 percent. He made the All-Star Team and dropped 41 points against the Sacramento Kings. And then came the playoff run, where he scored 22.9 points per contest, assisting at a rate of 6.5 per game and adding 5.1 rebounds.

The following seasons were nearly identical for Lillard. The 6-foot-3 point guard averaged nearly 36 minutes per night and routinely put up 20-plus points. (His points average climbed higher in 2015–16 to 25 points per contest.) In early December 2014, Lillard hit 7 of 11 from three-point land against the Chicago Bulls en route to a 35-point outing. Two games later versus the San Antonio Spurs, he hauled down 10 boards to go along with 23 points, 6 assists, 2 steals and a perfect 6 of 6 from the stripe. When the teams met again a week later, his 43 points led all scorers in a triple OT thriller. And those clutch stats? Through his first 14 career OT games, he made 29 of 41 field goals attempted (70.7 percent), 10 of 18 three-point field goals attempted (55.6 percent) and 15 of 16 free throws attempted (93.8 percent). Not bad performances to begin your career with.

In 2016–17 Lillard continued to prove he's one of the best in the league, despite not receiving an invitation to the 2017 All-Star Game. He finished sixth in scoring and in the top 10 for free-throw percentage. He punctuated the end of the season with a dazzling 59-point affair against the Utah

Jazz in which he drained 9 three-pointers. Lillard marched the Trail Blazers right back into the playoffs alongside another star-in-the-making, shooting guard C.J. McCollum. But up against a formidable opponent in the Golden State Warriors, the Blazers were swept despite Lillard's bold proclamation they could slay the former NBA champions.

Lillard, if you haven't realized, is a big-time budding star. If he can keep delivering, he'll continue sending fans in Rip City into a frenzy year after year.

CAREER HIGHLIGHTS

- Named NBA Rookie of the Year for 2012–13
- Named an NBA All-Rookie (First Team) in 2012–13
- Has played in two All-Star Games (2014, 2015)
- Placed sixth in NBA scoring (27.0) in 2016–17
- Led the Trail Blazers in points for two seasons (2015–16 and 2016–17)

KEVIN LOVE 0

A PRODUCT OF Lake Oswego High School in Oregon, Kevin Love was destined for the NBA. The prodigy took the west coast state by storm upon arriving in high school as a 6-foot-8 monster of a teenager. As a sophomore, he was a man among boys and once scored 50 points and 20 rebounds in one game. He led Lake Oswego to a state championship in his junior season, and during his final year, he averaged 33.9 points per game and 17 boards. That's what you call dominant.

Love's only year at UCLA was equally so. He accrued 17.5 points per game, 10.6 rebounds and a .565 field goal percentage while taking the Bruins to the 2008 Final Four alongside future NBA superstar Russell Westbrook. The Bruins lost to the Derrick Rose–led Memphis Tigers. It would be Love's only year at college, as he declared for the draft and was taken by the Memphis Grizzlies fifth overall. Subsequently traded to the Minnesota Timberwolves, he established himself quickly, becoming one of the scariest power forwards in the game under coach Rick Adelman.

At 6-foot-10 and 251 pounds, Love's inside strength is obvious and his rebounding prowess legendary. But it's also his deft touch from 20 feet out that makes him a threat from all points on the court. And when he gets to the line, he's shot 82 percent of his free throws thus far in his career. On November 12, 2010, history was made, and Love was the centerpiece. The power

forward hauled down 31 boards to go with 31 points against the New York Knicks. It was the first 30-30 game in the NBA in 28 years — since Moses Malone hit the mark in 1982. It was the most rebounds in a game since a guy named Charles Barkley accomplished the feat, and Love's teammate at the time, Michael Beasley, even claimed the big forward whispered to him Babe

Ruth–like on the bench, "I'm going for 30 tonight." Later that season he posted a line of 43 points and 17 boards, then smoothly followed that up with a 37-23 game. He led the NBA in rebounding in 2010–11 with 15.2 boards per game.

Despite Love's stellar play, the Timberwolves were a team in decline, and following 2013–14, when he put up arguably his best offensive season to date — 26.1 points, 12.5 boards and 4.4 assists (a career best) while shooting a respectable 45.7 percent from the field — Love made it known he wanted out.

Superstar LeBron James just happened to be making his own move, and Love became a focal point as the four-time MVP returned to Cleveland. James had played with Love in the 2012 Olympics and convinced his national squad teammate to forgo an offer to be a building block for the rebuilding Los Angeles Lakers and instead help him bring a championship to Cleveland.

With two number one picks in Andrew Wiggins and Anthony Bennett coming back to the Wolves in a three-team deal that also included Philadelphia, Love landed in Ohio with James, and the two of them joined crafty, bucket-slashing point guard Kyrie Irving to form the East's most explosive troika.

His first season in Cleveland, though, was a learning curve for Love — sharing the rock didn't come easily to the big man who likes to have the ball flow through him. Logically, playing with LeBron means Love's numbers have been down — and in some cases, such as points per game, way down. But he came to Ohio for one thing and one thing only — to win a ring. He put up 22 points and 19 boards versus Charlotte in December 2014 and routinely started going 20-10 after that. He finished the season with 38 double-doubles, tied for 10th most in 2014–15 and best on the Cavs.

A shoulder injury in the first round of the 2015 playoffs at the hands of Boston Celtics center Kelly Olynyk derailed Love's season, and he played no part in the Cavs' finals run that year. He did, however, play a pivotal role in Cleveland's 2016 title win the following season. In 2016–17 he averaged over 19 points and 11 rebounds per game, including a mammoth 39 points and 12 rebounds in a 140–135 OT win versus the Washington Wizards, one of the highest scoring and most entertaining games of the season. He made it known he'd be a force to be reckoned with early in

the Cavs' playoff run, posting 27 points and 11 rebounds (and going 11 for 11 from the charity stripe) in a Game 2 victory against the Indiana Pacers. He followed that up with 16 points and 14 boards in Game 3 of the second round versus Toronto as the Cavaliers continued making deep runs in the postseason.

The 28-year-old ball hawk has plenty of prime years left to establish a legacy as a multi-title winner in Ohio. When his contract expires in 2020, it will be money well spent to keep Love on board for the remainder of his career.

CAREER HIGHLIGHTS

- Named NBA Most Improved Player for 2010–11
- Named an NBA All-Rookie (Second Team) in 2008–09
- Has played in four All-Star Games (2011, 2012, 2014, 2017)
- Is second on the list of active NBA players for rebounds per game (11.5)
- Won an Olympic gold medal with the U.S. men's basketball team in London in 2012

POSITION SHOOTING GUARD / **SHOOTS** RIGHT / **HEIGHT** 6'7" / **WEIGHT** 215 LB. / **DRAFTED** 2011, GOLDEN STATE WARRIORS, 11TH OVERALL

KLAY THOMPSON 11

THE QUIETEST ONES are often the most dangerous — the deadly assassins who sneak up quietly to silence their enemies. Klay Thompson fits that mold perfectly. And don't think the laid-back west coaster is disinterested or nonplussed. He is a premier defender and a lights-out shooter who, in his short career, already holds some of the NBA's top shooting records. For the Golden State Warriors shooting guard, this is his prime time.

When Thompson set the NBA record for most points in one quarter with 37, we should have known it would be only the first of many jaw-dropping moments. It was as if Thompson channeled the catchphrase "he's on fire" from the old video game *NBA Jam*. When he's firing a shot, defenders need to look out. It could be from deep, or from the corner or off the dribble, but it's usually nothing but net. After that 37-point third quarter in early 2015, the shooting guard dropped a cool 60 points in just 29 minutes the following season against Indiana, nearly matching Kobe Bryant's 62 points in three quarters. But even that's nothing compared with Game 6 in the 2016 Western Conference finals. Facing elimination and down in the fourth quarter in Oklahoma City, Golden State turned to Klay. He made it rain, dropping 11 three-pointers — the most ever in a playoff game — en route to 41 points and the win, which launched the Warriors back into the NBA Finals.

- Named an NBA All-Rookie (First Team) in 2011–12
- Has played in three All-Star Games (2015–2017)
- Won the NBA Three-Point Contest in 2016
- Set an NBA record for most points scored in one quarter (37) in 2015
- Won an Olympic gold medal with the U.S. men's basketball team in Rio in 2016

three seasons and averaging 21.6 points his final year. After being drafted 11th overall by Golden State, Thompson took his talents to California, where he's been happy to play second fiddle for a perennial championship team. That doesn't mean he doesn't want to get his due when he's feeling it, as we've seen again and again with Thompson. There may be no player in the league who can score in waves like he can.

Like Curry's father, Dell, Thompson's father, Mychal, was a pro basketball player in the 1980s, the first overall pick in the 1978 draft who suited up with the Portland Trail Blazers, the San Antonio Spurs and the LA Lakers, winning two titles late in his career. He's now a radio broadcaster for the Lakers. "He's my biggest believer," Thompson said about his father in 2014. "He always told me . . . that I could make it to the NBA if I just stayed humble and worked hard."

The quiet superstar has a contract with the Warriors through to 2019, making over $17 million per season. He also has two NBA championship rings, an Olympic gold medal and several entries in the NBA record book because of his shooting performances. His father always wanted him to be a Laker, but with the way things are going, Thompson may be a Warrior for life.

That's what you call heat check, and it likely played a role in Kevin Durant's abandoning a title dream in Oklahoma and joining Thompson and the Golden State Warriors the following season.

Thompson owes some of his success to the all-star cast around him who take the pressure off. Cover Steph Curry and you leave Klay wide open. Then there's former MVP Durant waiting for the rock to drive it to the hoop. It means Thompson can lurk in the shadows, bide his time and spend a ton of energy at the other end of the court guarding the opposing team's best shooter.

The 6-foot-7, 215-pound shooting guard is the perfect blend of size and speed. Thompson's durability is something to

behold — he rarely gets hurt and rarely takes a night off defensively. If pouring his energy into his defense means he must sacrifice points, so be it. He's got a former MVP named Steph Curry in the backcourt to pick up the offensive slack.

In 2014–15 he set career highs in free-throw and three-point percentages with 88 percent from the line and 44 percent from behind the arc. He seized the Three-Point Contest win at the 2016 All-Star Game in Toronto, and in 2016–17 he set a career-high average in points with 22.3 per game.

Raised in Lake Oswego, Oregon, where he played alongside future NBAer Kevin Love, Thompson was the toast of the town at the University of Washington, playing

JOHN WALL 2

SOME PLAYERS JUST can't seem to get a fair shake — they are good, even great, but perhaps not superstar great. That could be a product of playing in a certain era, or simply the fault of high expectations. Either way, John Wall's firmly been in the category of not getting enough respect. And that's about to change.

Wall's as pure a point guard as they come: lightning-quick first step, excellent shot, deadly passer. The latter was

especially true in the 2014–15 season when he started averaging 10 assists per game en route to a starting All-Star appearance (his second at the time). With Wall's leadership, the Washington Wizards are firmly a playoff contender. Teammates like Bradley Beal and Marcin Gortat don't hurt either, but it's Wall's magic that stokes the engine of the team, and he's finally getting his due.

The 6-foot-4 guard didn't have a typical childhood — his father was incarcer-

ated just after John was born and passed away when he was just nine. Wall was a tempestuous kid on and off the court in his hometown of Raleigh, North Carolina, and the kids took to calling him "Crazy J." Anger issues made several coaches ban him from high-level basketball camps when he was a teenager. But he finally got his act together, and by the time he graduated, he led his team to the state championship, averaging 19.7 points, 9 assists and just over 8 rebounds. His speed is undeniable, Iverson-esque, and his high school coach claims he clocked him at 3.5 seconds from end line to end line when Wall was still a teenager.

He was a one-and-done at the University of Kentucky, putting up 16.6 points and 6.5 dimes per contest before he was selected first overall by the Wizards in the 2010 draft. He recorded a triple-double six games into his rookie season (19 points, 13 assists and 10 rebounds), but the Wizards were simply horrible, losing 59 games. They lost 46 in the lockout-shortened 2011–12 season and 59 again the following year. Some players may have gotten used to all the losing. Not Wall. Not a kid who came from the rough Raleigh projects like he did. It might be hard to imagine such a once-selfish person on the basketball court becoming one of the league's most unselfish players. But that is exactly what Wall did — and how he led the Wizards out of the NBA hinterlands.

He's averaging more than 9 assists per game during his career and has emerged as a basketball player masquerading as an artist: he drives down the lane and spins 360 for layups; throws behind-the-back passes to teammates; startles opponents with a "yo-yo" dribble and a fake pass that creates space for him and his teammates.

He began the 2014–15 season with two 30-point affairs in the first five games. In December he recorded 17 assists twice and started that month with seven straight games of 10-plus assists, putting up only one game of fewer than 8 helpers. Or how about his 28 points, 12 assists and 8 rebounds in January against Toronto? By the All-Star break, he was leading the team in points, assists and steals, the same as he did in 2013–14. It's hard to imagine where the Wizards would be without the former Kentucky product hoisting this team on his back, especially in the first round of the 2015 playoffs, when he torched the Toronto Raptors during a four-game sweep. But a wrist fracture at the beginning of the second round forced him to the bench, and despite a valiant return later in the series, the Wizards were bounced by the Atlanta Hawks. The team failed to make the postseason the following year, but Wall continued his ascension into the upper stratosphere of the NBA. Named Eastern Conference Player of the Month in December 2015, he followed up that honor with four triple-doubles in the second half of the season despite carrying bumps and bruises along the way.

In 2016–17, after surgery on both knees, Wall saw his points per game climb three points while still maintaining the second highest assist rate in the NBA. Highlights included a 14-point, 20-assist game against Chicago late in the season and a ridiculous 41 points, 8 assists and 7 rebounds against the LA Clippers two weeks later. Washington defeated the Atlanta Hawks in the first round of the playoffs, with Wall's 42 points, 8 assists and 4 steals in Game 6 the final nail in the coffin. His performance in the second round was just as epic: in Game 6 against the Boston Celtics, with Washing-

ton facing elimination, Wall hit a game-winning three-pointer that sent the home crowd into a frenzy and forced a Game 7 in Boston, which they lost.

Long gone is the ghost of Gilbert Arenas, a one-time superstar with a massive contract who fizzled out in Washington. In his stead is the man with quick hands and faster feet, who has quietly become one of the best guards in the game today and who just might bring Washington its first championship in over 35 years.

CAREER HIGHLIGHTS

- Named an NBA All-Rookie (First Team) in 2010–11
- Named to NBA All-Defensive Second Team in 2014–15
- Has played in four All-Star Games (2014–2017)
- Drafted by the Washington Wizards in the first round (1st overall) in 2010
- Ranks second in assists per game (9.2) among active NBA players

THE DUNK CONTEST

ON FEBRUARY 9, 1991, it's fair to say few inside the Charlotte Coliseum had heard of a 6-foot shooting guard named Dee Brown. In the past, winners of the NBA Slam Dunk Contest — stars such as Dominique Wilkins, Michael Jordan and Spud Webb, who would define their early careers with the exposure at the annual All-Star Game — were already known to the masses. Not so for the Celtics rookie. When the unknown shooting guard leaned down, pumped up his Reebok shoes and leapt toward the basket with one arm draped over his eyes, he entered NBA lore, winning the 1991 dunk contest with the now-famous no-look dunk. Immediately immortalized thereafter on posters and in magazines, the jam heard 'round the world prompted Magic Johnson to say on air that February night: "Everybody at home, don't try that. That is unbelievable." The dunk is so iconic that Brown's daughter, now a college basketball player

Zach LaVine, the 2015 dunk champ, slams under the spotlight during the 2015 competition.

Dee Brown drapes his arm over his eyes for a no-look jam at the 1991 Slam Dunk Contest. The creative dunk won Brown the contest and made him an instant sensation.

herself, cannot escape questions about her father's moment in the spotlight nearly 25 years ago.

More so than Jordan's stretch slam from the foul line, Wilkins' windmill or Vince Carter's between the legs, Brown's no-looker sent the dunk contest to another stratosphere and etched his name on the lips of young fans for years down the road. A vital change had occurred: no longer was the evening designed for a select group of well-known individuals. No longer was it a superstar's athleticism shining through. Dee Brown was just a kid, an everyman, wearing second-tier shoes and flashing a Gumby flattop haircut. His creative, organic flair began an era at the All-Star Game that encouraged out-of-box thinking, something that would become a trademark for the next generation of NBA players for years to come.

IN THE (NEAR) BEGINNING

The name Larry Nance likely conjures up a whole lot of . . . diddly squat. But in 1984, Nance was named the winner of the first NBA Slam Dunk Contest, edging out the legendary Julius Erving for the $10,000 prize. The contestants that year in Denver were a ragtag group — legends like Erving, unheralded middle-of-the-road 80s NBA stars like Darrell Griffith and Michael Cooper, and a few off-the-map rookies. It was a motley crew to say the least.

As for marquee stars, Dr. J was already a household name inside and outside the league, nearing the end of his career. He gained early fame for his history-altering dunk from the free-throw line in 1976 at the ABA All-Star Game, the first dunk contest of its kind, also held in Denver, and he was widely known around the NBA for spectacular in-game slams. Atlanta Hawks stud Dominique Wilkins — drafted third overall in the 1982 draft — was still young but already making a name for himself as a power-slamming specialist known as "the Human Highlight Film." Trail Blazers guard Clyde "the Glide" Drexler may have been a first-year player and unknown outside the Portland area, but anyone who followed his career in college knew he was a product of "Phi Slama Jama," the Houston

squad that defined their team around lob plays and high-flying dunks. (To all those Clippers fans, that's the original Lob City.) Then there was all 7-foot-4 of Ralph Sampson, the former Rookie of the Year and the tallest player in the competition. The judges were equally offbeat and included a Colorado congresswoman and a New York Mets catcher.

Dr. J was the man to beat of course, and in 2014, Darrell Griffith (whose nickname was Dr. Dunkenstein) said: "[Erving] still had hops. He had them bear claw hands. He could grab the ball like it was an orange." Fan participation included scribbling numbers on handmade cards to rate dunks, something that gained in popularity as time went on, becoming a staple in the stands and at the judges table as the contest progressed. And although Nance may have been proclaimed the winner by points — and bought a Camaro with his

Dr. J is in full flight at the first-ever professional slam dunk competition, which took place at the 1976 ABA All-Star Game. Dr. J won the competition with this jam that started from the free-throw line.

man on the court, seconds before he leaps in the air, trying something no one has ever dared attempt. It is the moment where "what if?" becomes reality.

THE LAST GREAT DUNK

The 1990s following Dee Brown's signature slam was a largely forgettable era of dunking, and by the time Brent Barry — AKA the only white guy to ever win the Slam Dunk Contest — was declared the winner in 1996, times had truly changed. The NBA shelved the contest for several years in a bid to regroup, and then along came Vince Carter.

The North Carolina product was a second-year player for the Toronto Raptors in 2000, the year the dunk contest ticked upward once again. That season, the fifth overall pick from the 1998 draft averaged a career-high 25.7 points per game, leading the young Raps into the playoffs for the first time in franchise history. Carter was a throwback to the old dunkers — a fluid mix of creativity, raw power and ingenuity that immediately launched him into the mix of the greatest to ever slam. His between-the-legs midair jam to claim the title vaulted him to the top of the dunking charts. Up until 2014–15, when youngster Zach LaVine wowed the crowd, many casual fans, and LaVine himself, would say Carter was the last great dunker thanks to a plethora of moves that included a 360 windmill, an elbow in the rim and the aforementioned between-the-legs dunk. What's undeniable is that night in DC has been etched in NBA lore and is still dubbed "the last great dunk contest."

With the passage of time and Carter now a 40-year-old veteran playing out his career in Memphis, many have looked back on what that dunk symbolized for the entire country of Canada. He was quickly named "Air Canada," and "Vinsanity" arrived full force north of the border. It was a marketer's dream, much the same as when Reebok captured the zeitgeist of Dee Brown. The Raptors were desperately seeking legitimacy after a series of losing seasons to begin their tenure. Carter provided that, and if not for a game-ending clanker in the seventh contest of the Raptors' 2001 second-round playoff series versus the Allen Iverson–led Philadelphia 76ers, Toronto may have done some damage in the Eastern Conference that year.

What no one could have predicted was that a young generation of Canadian basketball fans would gravitate to Carter like moths to a flame. Soon they would be attempting Carter's awe-inspiring slams when they got older. In late 2014, Carter was honored during the first quarter of a Grizzlies–Raptors game. He looked back on his time in Toronto and the impact it had on the fans. "All of a sudden, after that first playoff win . . . everybody wanted to pick up a basketball. It was fantastic," he said. Among those fans: a seven-year-old Nik Stauskas, a Mississauga native and now a Philadelphia 76er, and a five-year-old Andrew Wiggins, 2014–15 Rookie of the Year and the heir apparent to the Carter legend. Carter's own hero was Dr. J, and although the doctor may have inspired a legion of dunk enthusiasts, he didn't impact an entire nation like Carter.

winnings — the moment of the night belonged to Erving when he revisited his '76 ABA slam by running the length of the floor, leaping from behind the charity stripe once again and scoring the first perfect score of the night. The crowd went wild. "The whole show was just a buildup for Dr. J," contestant Michael Cooper said years later. "You could feel the electricity in the gym."

Jordan would re-create Dr. J's dunk several years later in 1988 — it too immortalized poster form, perhaps even one that Dee Brown had in his room. Posters were currency in the pre-Internet NBA, street cred for the athletically inclined teenager, a way to show off one's allegiance to a team or a newfound hero who could do amazing things with a basketball. Those posters of high-flying heroes showing off their moves in the dunk contest populated the bedrooms of basketball fans years before kids traded in still images for YouTube videos.

Although the modern-day dunk competition may have morphed into more spectacle than contest — with cool sneakers and trick dunks the norm — there's something still exciting about seeing one

IN THE BEGINNING

The origins of dunking date back to the early part of the 20th century. A *New York Times* writer described Joe Fortenberry, the captain of the 1936 U.S. men's basketball team, as "pitch[ing] the ball downward into the hoop, much like a cafeteria customer dunking a roll in coffee." Although this may have popularized the term nationally, dunk was in fact used to describe the play of stuffing the ball in the hoop in several other smaller newspapers prior to the *Times* during the early part of the 1930s. (Los Angeles Lakers play-by-play announcer Chick Hearn, who voiced the team for 42 years before his death in 2002, is widely acknowledged as creating the saying "slam dunk" with specificity to Wilt Chamberlain.) For years following, many in the game, from general managers to coaches, tried to eliminate dunking, or at the very least, raise the

Michael Jordan pays homage to Dr. J and his legendary 1976 charity-stripe slam with his own dunk from the stripe at the 1988 Slam Dunk Contest.

rim to 12 feet to thwart the practice. An underlying subtext, especially by the 1950s and 1960s, was more than likely the increasing number of African-American players in the game and their ability to dunk more often than their white counterparts. Beyond any racial subtext, the prevailing opinion was that as players were getting taller, dunking was changing the game, and in 1940, one American wrote: "Many people claim that there is no premium on accuracy. That instead of beautiful shooting, slap happy basketball has resulted with wild throwing from every possible angle calculated to get the ball into range of the backboards where the skyscraper boys bat it down for two points."

The three-point line that emerged in the NBA in 1979, basketball's version of a home run, was a direct response to a league that had changed, especially with the likes of massive centers skilled in the art of slamming, including Kareem Abdul-Jabbar, Bill Russell and Chamberlain. The NCAA even banned dunking for nearly a decade following Abdul-Jabbar's dominance at UCLA in the 60s, when he won three straight national championships, compiling a record of 88-2. Adding a three-point line — thanks to pressure and ingenuity from ABA commish George Mikan in 1967 — lengthened the game, creating a faster, more up-tempo pace that took the focus away from the paint and allowed guards to flourish. What we see today is a guard-heavy game that's focused on hitting an open man for three in transition, or moving the ball around the perimeter to find an open shot, rather than feeding a big man like Abdul-Jabbar in the paint.

MODERN-DAY DUNKS

But it's not raining threes for everyone. Just ask Zach LaVine. In 2015, a much-needed uplift occurred in the dunking department thanks to the jaw-dropping performance of the 19-year-old shooting guard. In an age where posters are obsolete and six-second Internet videos and flashing GIFs appear mere moments after a live play, the rising star did not disappoint. He confidently donned a No. 23 Michael Jordan jersey and mimicked a Space Jam dunk, going through the legs and up for a reverse one-hander. It was sick. He flipped the ball in the air again on the second attempt and then went around his own back in midair, perhaps the most innovative of his four dunks. LaVine had the select group of NBA All-Stars flying out of their seats in amazement. For a contest that desperately needed a shot in the arm after several lackluster years — Dr. J had said the year prior, "You might never get back to the day when you've got the two best players in the league . . . facing off, like you did in the heyday" — LaVine delivered, at least in terms of a solo effort. Was it on par with Carter, Erving, Wilkins and MJ? Quite possibly. LaVine has called Carter "the best dunker of all time." But now, at the very least, the kid deserves to be mentioned with the greats, particularly since the contest itself has suffered some growing pains throughout the last decade and because he repeated as champion the following year in an unforgettable back-and-forth duel with Orlando's Aaron Gordon. In fact, LaVine's battle with Gordon is being hailed as one of the best contests in years, with LaVine just escaping defeat thanks to a flying one-hander from just before the free-throw line. Gordon, for his part, had the dunk of the night, leaping over a mascot and going under the legs for a left-handed jam.

So what is it exactly about LaVine's (or, for that matter, Gordon's) performances that stand out? That "wow" factor. All great dunkers have it. A sense of showmanship, talent and raw power all wrapped into one. Sure, Dwight Howard's Superman cape in 2008 was fun, but was it awe-inspiring? Hardly. Steve Nash's soccer header to Amar'e Stoudemire was crafty and clever, but come on. Gerald Green blowing out a candle in 2007 on a cupcake was kind of hard?

Two-time dunk champion Dominique Wilkins, known for his aggressive rim-shaking slams, pounds this ball down at the 1988 Slam Dunk Contest.

Was it really that cool when 5-foot-9 Nate Robinson launched himself over former winner Spud Webb? Sure, for a half-second and for the sheer fact he could elevate that high. Robinson — a three-time dunk contest champ, who also jumped over the aforementioned Howard — undoubtedly wowed the crowd. But something beyond simple elevation is needed to capture the imagination of the fans and become legendary. (Arguably, Webb's two-handed reverse in 1986, after lobbing the ball in the air 10-plus feet, was purer in form and 20 years earlier. Plus, he was only 5-foot-7, and watching Webb spring from an average man's height to the rim is pure theater.)

Like Webb's gravity-defying leap, the greatest dunks in the history of the contest have always been simple in concept, difficult in execution, pure in power. Take Wilkins, "the Human Highlight Film," two-time winner of the dunk contest, one in 1985, another in 1990. In '85, up against his longtime dunking rival, Jordan, Wilkins' windmill dunk helped secure his status as an elite player and put the Hawks on the map. Forever in the shadow of the Bulls star —

Zach LaVine pays homage to both Michael Jordan and Vince Carter with his Toon Squad through-the-legs slam that helped him win the 2015 title.

he consistently finished second in league scoring to MJ — that was one night where Wilkins came out on top. In 2015, Wilkins described his own style as bringing an element of "flare and power to the dunk contest." The Hawks star certainly did that in '85.

Although Jordan would go on to defeat Wilkins famously in 1988 by launching himself from (almost) the charity stripe à la Dr. J, because the All-Star weekend occurred in Chicago, many, including Wilkins, believed MJ's perfect score for his final dunk was blatant home favoritism. Wilkins, in 2014, even acknowledged in an interview that the famously competitive Jordan once told him: "You probably won. You know it, I know it. But we're in Chicago. What can I tell you?" Wilkins went on to say that of the five dunk contests he participated in, he "won four, but got credit for two." All said, it was a natural rivalry from two great competitors of the game, and something rarely seen in the modern era, particularly as many competitors now are rookies or up-and-coming stars in the league without much history. Who knows — maybe the Gordon–LaVine rivalry is just beginning.

SO WHERE DO we go from here? LaVine may have changed the game going forward, incorporating old-style dunks with a modern twist and making us all forget about the recent exploits of Robinson and Howard. In a clip that aired before the 2015 contest, a young LaVine discussed his early obsession with watching old dunk contests, particularly Jordan, something Carter admitted to doing as well. It showed, and maybe that's the way to a new era — look to the past. Kids need to be inspired by individuals, not spoon-fed by the league, and the NBA has done an excellent job of identifying superstars, or dunking artists like LaVine, and marketing them to fans. (Perhaps that's why NBA superstars have 10 times more Twitter followers than baseball players.)

Moving forward, the contest will likely oscillate between the gimmicky approach and a pure, no-holds-barred one that feels more like something that would happen organically on the playground. (Your honor, we present exhibit number one in the gimmicky category from the 2017 dunk contest: DeAndre Jordan grabbing the ball from DJ Khaled and leaping over an entire DJ booth.) While Dr. J's 1976 free-throw dunk looks relatively pedestrian to modern-day jammers, watching him palm the ball, back up and run the length of the court, and leap from the line was a sight to behold back then; it was pure spectacle, akin to something Evel Knievel might have pulled off. The thrill of the improbable is where the dunk contest should reside. When Dee Brown pumped up his Reeboks, he set the stage, and from there he simply leaned down, took off and covered his eyes while the world held its breath.

DIRK NOWITZKI

POSITION SMALL FORWARD / **SHOOTS** RIGHT / **HEIGHT** 6'11" / **WEIGHT** 222 LB. / **DRAFTED** 2013, MILWAUKEE BUCKS, 15TH OVERALL

GIANNIS ANTETOKOUNMPO 34

WHEN YOU'VE GOT a nickname like "the Greek Freak," there's bound to be something special about the way you play. That's exactly the case with Giannis Antetokounmpo, the Milwaukee Bucks star who is tearing up the NBA with an insane combination of length, speed and talent with the ball.

Born to Nigerian parents but raised in Athens, Antetokounmpo grew up poor and hungry, sharing basketball sneakers with his brother Thanasis — the two even hawked souvenirs to tourists to help pay the bills. "When we were playing basketball, [we forgot] everything that [was] happening to us," Thanasis said in 2014. Giannis, who was scouted at 13, began plying his trade in a low-level second-division Greek league (what one NBA exec deemed "YMCA level") before reaching the pinnacle of basketball. Given his visibility on YouTube it may feel like the 6-foot-11 small forward has been in the NBA for years, but 2016–17 was only the fourth full season for the 15th overall pick of the 2013 draft, who's since become a human highlight reel night in, night out.

The excitable international star recorded his first career double-double several months into his rookie year, going 16 and 10 against the Brooklyn Nets. By January, he was regularly putting up double-digit figures in points, and his minutes were dramatically increasing, a great sign for a rookie who clearly was picking up on the finer points of the game. Instead of getting buried on the bench, Antetokounmpo was playing 25 to 30 minutes a night for a young Bucks squad focused on creating a winner. For many fans, their first large-scale introduction to the high-flying Greek was at the 2015 Slam Dunk Contest. The Freak walked out into Madison Square Garden with a procession of flower-haired women and the Greek flag draped over his shoulders — not a shabby entrance. But the competition quickly showed that Antetokounmpo's in-game dunks are more exciting than the uncontested jams thrown down in exhibition.

When it comes to games that count, Antetokounmpo's crafty Eurostep move — sometimes started beyond the free-throw line — allows him to get to the basket

quickly and slam on surprised players. His length is nearly impossible to guard, his wingspan stretching like a bird of prey in midflight. Although he wasn't a rebounding machine in his first few seasons — he's slender and agile, and more a scorer than a defender — he's proven that he's certainly capable of getting up on the glass and helping out, as evidenced by the 8.8 boards he averaged in 2016–17. He can also be a help defender by launching in the air against smaller players, and he's added almost 2 blocks per game to his arsenal, including 4 stuffs against the Indiana Pacers early in 2015 and 7, count 'em, 7, blocks against the Charlotte Hornets on the final day of 2016. He may not shoot the three consistently yet — a must for big men these days — but those skills will come once he develops the fundamentals needed to play in the NBA at a high level. And that's happening; in March 2016 the Greek Freak put up 26 points, 12 boards and 10 assists and added

3 steals and 4 blocks for one of his most versatile and well-rounded games that season. In February 2017, Antetokounmpo dropped a career-high 41 points in a loss to the LA Lakers, proving he possesses the skill set to be a go-to offensive weapon up front.

The Bucks made the playoffs in 2016–17 and are building a nucleus around the Greek prodigy, as well as 2014's number two overall pick Jabari Parker. Antetokounmpo's 2016–17 per-game line of 22.9 points, 8.8 rebounds, 5.4 assists, 1.9 blocks and 1.6 steals was mind-blowing — one of just a handful of players in NBA history to lead his team in all five categories and place top 20 in the league in those same categories. He plays several positions on the court, giving the Bucks a lot of looks depending on their lineup, and is well on his way to becoming one of the NBA's next superstars, as evidenced by that 41-point game and the multiple triple-doubles he stamped on the scoresheet.

CAREER HIGHLIGHTS

- Named NBA Most Improved Player for 2016–17
- Named an NBA All-Rookie (Second Team) in 2013–14
- Played in the NBA All-Star Game in 2017
- Was an All-NBA Second Team selection for 2016–17
- Drafted by the Milwaukee Bucks in the first round (15th overall) in 2013

Given enough time, Antetokounmpo may launch himself into the conversation as one of the best international players in the history of the game, alongside stalwarts Dirk Nowitzki and Tim Duncan. He's certain to be the best basketball product to ever come out of the tiny nation of Greece — a once-in-a-generation talent who seems poised to take the basketball world by storm.

POSITION POINT GUARD–SHOOTING GUARD / **SHOOTS** LEFT / **HEIGHT** 6'3" / **WEIGHT** 190 LB. / **DRAFTED** 2008, SAN ANTONIO SPURS, 45TH OVERALL

GORAN DRAGIC 7

EUROPE HAS BECOME a hotbed for NBA talent the past decade, and perhaps no player better exemplifies that basketball truly is an international sport than Goran Dragic, who hails from the tiny country of Slovenia. He's emerged as one of the best guards in the game, and after several successful seasons in Phoenix, he's now the starting point guard for the Miami Heat.

After an injury derailed his budding career on the soccer field, Dragic turned to the hardcourt. He was immediately hooked, waking up at 3:00 a.m. to watch NBA stars such as Michael Jordan and Allen Iverson. In 2012 he said, "Inside my blood, I love basketball." He tore up the Slovenian league as a youngster and helped lead the U-20 team to a gold medal at the 2004 FIBA championship. Dragic was drafted 45th overall in 2008 by the San Antonio Spurs but was quickly swapped to the Suns. He started slowly, coming off the bench his first three seasons in Phoenix. "I was not aggressive enough," he said, looking back at his early years. His coach told him to forget about the mistakes, but it took a while to sink in. He had an especially difficult time dealing with the larger NBA shot-blockers.

Midway through his third season, the Slovenian was moved to Houston, where he earned backup minutes while continuing to put up respectable numbers. The following season, Dragic finally started, and in 66 games that year posted what at

that point was his best line — 11.7 points per game, 5.3 assists and a career-high 80.5 percent from the stripe.

As a free agent, the point guard returned to Phoenix, where he was given the chance

to start — flourishing as one of the top players in the game at his position. His numbers in 2013–14 were a career best; 20.3 points per game, 5.9 assists and a smooth .505 field goal percentage helped

- Named NBA Most Improved Player for 2013–14
- Was an All-NBA Third Team selection for 2013–14
- Is a member of the NBA's 20-50-40 club (points, FG %, 3PT %)
- Is a two-time NBA Player of the Week
- Is a two-time Stankovic Cup champion with Slovenia (2007, 2010)

Dragic emerge as one of the purest shooters in the NBA. He was deadly from behind the arc, converting chances at more than 40 percent — and his defense was good too, with 1.4 steals per contest.

Dragic's go-to move is a nearly unstoppable step-back jumper that is difficult to guard effectively. He sets up the shot by dribbling hard right before launching backward off his left foot to give him separation from his defender and a clean look at the bucket. The shot is very similar to that of fellow international star Dirk Nowitzki, who's used it to climb into the NBA's top-10 all-time scorers. It helps that Dragic is a natural lefty, another difference maker in his game that makes him difficult to defend.

In 2013–14 he had several monster games, in early December dropping 34 against the Pacers, followed by 28 points and 13 dimes against the Mavericks, powering Phoenix to wins in both contests. Nearing the trade deadline, the Suns had a logjam at point guard and ended up dealing Dragic and his younger brother, Zoran (who joined the Suns at the beginning of 2014–15 and played sparingly in his first stint in the NBA), to Miami for picks and veteran role players. Dragic finished the year with 16.3 points per game, 4.5 helpers and 3.5 rebounds; in his 26-game sample with Miami, he continued to play well, improving to 80 percent from the stripe and

5.3 assists per game. He signed a five-year, $90 million deal to stay in Florida.

Dragic's shifty moves and pure jumping ability are two assets that add several different looks to the Heat offense. He's a pure point guard and a key piece the team has been missing since the LeBron James/Dwyane Wade/Chris Bosh years. In Wade's final year in Miami, Dragic led the team to Game 7 of the second round in the 2016 playoffs. The series included a 30-point game versus the Toronto Raptors that forced the final game.

Pairing Dragic with center Hassan Whiteside, the Heat overcame an awful 11-30 start in the 2016–17 season to nearly steal the eighth seed, which opened the NBA's eyes to a well-coached young crop of hopefuls and a group of savvy vets led by Dragic. He ended the year with 20.3 points, 5.8 assists and 40.5 percent three-point shooting in 73 games.

For the point guard from across the world, just making it to the NBA is a success story. Competing at the highest level is a whole different ball game.

PAU GASOL 16

ONE OF THE best international centers in the game, Spanish native Pau Gasol has helped redefine the position along with another European, Dirk Nowitzki. And while Gasol may not have the step-back three like the German, his post moves are second to none. After a solid first season with the San Antonio Spurs (his 16th), Gasol's hoping to add one more ring to his collection as his career winds down.

Growing up in Barcelona, Gasol was a natural. Seven feet tall before his college years, he destroyed opponents with a crafty mix of agility and touch to go along with his size. He received the MVP award in the 2001 Spanish King's Cup and was soon playing for the Spanish national team. "He totally exploded and took over. It was pretty unbelievable," recalled his younger brother Marc, himself an All-NBA center.

Pau went third overall in the 2001 draft to the Atlanta Hawks, who immediately traded him to the Memphis Grizzlies for Shareef Abdur-Rahim. The entire Gasol family moved to Tennessee. There, Gasol won 2002 Rookie of the Year. He subsequently spent seven seasons with the Grizzlies, the same team Marc now plays for — they were, in fact, traded for each other. Although the Grizz made the playoffs three years in a row, they never advanced past the first round. Pau took the heat in the south for being soft, and after a foot injury at the 2006 FIBA World Championship sidelined him, his play

suffered. He was traded in early 2008 to the LA Lakers in a blockbuster deal that changed everything.

From playing 1A and going to 1B behind Kobe Bryant, Pau made a splash in California, winning two titles with the Lakers. His first full year in LA, Gasol was a beast — his 18.9 points and 9.6 rebounds while playing 37 minutes a night gave the Lakers an offensive boost and gave Bryant the room he needed to operate. Gasol posted similar numbers in the playoffs and tasted victory in the finals over the Orlando Magic, besting Dwight Howard down low.

In each of their title runs, Gasol logged 40 minutes a game, and he averaged more than 20 points and 10 rebounds the year the Lakers repeated, with the Barcelona native hauling down 18 boards in the deciding Game 7 versus the Boston Celtics.

But with Bryant winding down and a failed experiment with Steve Nash, Gasol entered free agency in 2014 and elected to take his talents to Chicago where he teamed up with former MVP Derrick Rose and former Defensive Player of the Year Joakim Noah. His first season in Chitown was a rebirth for Gasol. He hauled down nearly 12 rebounds a game, a career high and good for fourth overall in the league.

Contributing 18.5 points per game and 2 blocks revealed how well he played at both ends of the floor, particularly with Rose injured at times. Perhaps no better way to describe the center's worth is the 54 double-doubles he put up while playing against younger, stronger men. He also had the fifth-most assists per game among forwards that season, a testament to his adaptability and ability to read the double team when it comes.

Gasol's well known for his cultural pursuits and is highly intelligent off the court. He speaks numerous languages — he and Bryant used to speak Spanish together on the court to confuse opponents — and he maintains a strong interest in medicine, taking after his mother, who is a doctor.

His consistency and durability are impressive. He's been an All-Star six times, starting alongside his brother in 2015, the first time in the NBA that's ever happened. He can pass, shoot and run the floor gracefully. In the paint, Gasol's difficult to defend against. A smooth midrange jumper, his strong post-up and up-and-down head fakes give opponents headaches.

He played one more season in Chicago before electing to replace Tim Duncan in Texas. Though he played fewer minutes

- Named NBA Rookie of the Year for 2001–02
- Named an NBA All-Rookie (First Team) in 2001–02
- Has played in six All-Star Games (2006, 2009–2011, 2015–2016)
- Registered his 20,000th point at the end of 2016–17
- Won an Olympic silver medal with the Spanish men's basketball team in London in 2012

(and did not start every game) alongside LaMarcus Aldridge in San Antonio, Gasol's leadership was instrumental in guiding the Spurs to a 61-21 record in 2016–17. Gasol finished the season with a respectable 12.4 points and 7.8 boards. These numbers may be down from previous years and well off his career averages, but the veteran's presence counts for so much more beyond the boxscore, and the Spurs made the Western Conference finals despite key injuries to Tony Parker and Kawhi Leonard.

Can the talented Spurs once again dominate the Western Conference? Only time will tell. Gasol has two rings already — a third, at 37 years of age or more, would cement a legacy.

POSITION SHOOTING GUARD / **SHOOTS** LEFT / **HEIGHT** 6'6" / **WEIGHT** 205 LB. / **DRAFTED** 1999, SAN ANTONIO SPURS, 57TH OVERALL

MANU GINOBILI [20]

IT'S HARD TO imagine a basketball player having an impact in the NBA when he is nearly 40 — especially a shooting guard whose position dictates lots of slashing and driving play. And yet, Argentine star Manu Ginobili, whose body has taken a beating over the years thanks to his style of play,

keeps on ticking. He's still pounding the rock inside to San Antonio's bigs; still driving to the basket and throwing up a prayer before falling to the floor; still stepping off a screen and taking a pass from Tony Parker. As part of the three-headed international triad in San Antonio that included the

legendary Tim Duncan, Ginobili will go down as one of the most influential international players in the NBA.

Emanuel Ginobili was drafted 57th overall in 1999. The Spurs fleeced the NBA with their international scouting that year, and it wouldn't be the first time or the last. They already had top pick Duncan, selected in 1997 (from the U.S. Virgin Islands), and they identified Tony Parker (of France) several years later deep in the first round. The Spurs would dominate for the next decade with their internationally born trio.

Ginobili was a huge star in his home country before bolting to Italy. There he played with Kinder Bologna and was named the Euroleague Finals MVP in 2000–01 before crossing the pond and getting his first taste of NBA action as a 25-year-old.

He started just five games his rookie season for San Antonio, averaging 7.6 points and 2 assists per game while playing for a deep Spurs squad. His impact was felt more in the playoffs, and the Argentine offered a skilled weapon off the bench as the Spurs cruised to victory in the 2003 NBA Finals. It would be their first of three NBA championships in five years. In 2004–05, en route to the second ring, Ginobili started 74 games, knocking down per-game totals of 16 points, 4.4 rebounds and 3.9 assists while shooting 80 percent from the stripe and nearly 38 percent from behind the arc. During the title run, he upped

CAREER HIGHLIGHTS

- Named NBA Sixth Man of the Year for 2007–08
- Named an NBA All-Rookie (Second Team) in 2002–03
- Has played in two All-Star Games (2005, 2011)
- Is a three-time All-NBA Third Team selection (2007–08, 2010–2011)
- Won an Olympic gold medal with the Argentine men's basketball team in Athens in 2004 and a bronze in Beijing in 2008

(a career high) in a season that included back-to-back 37-point efforts early and a season-high 46 against Cleveland in a 112–105 win on 15-of-20 shooting, 8 of which were three-pointers. It was this ability to get hot and take over games that endeared him to fans and pushed San Antonio over the top when needed. He started just 23 of 74 games yet played 31 minutes per contest on average, which makes that season even more miraculous.

Ginobili's no-holds-barred type of guard play — attacking the rim on offense in a controlled yet reckless manner, while his defense is characterized by a scrappy max effort—paved the way for the current era of superstar guards. Would James Harden exist if Ginobili hadn't been allowed to thrive?

All those extra playoff games and hard-fought minutes added a lot of mileage over the years to Ginobili's legs. In 2016–17 it looked as though he may have lost a step, but he was still effective. He played 69 games coming off the bench and a stalwart 18.7 minutes per contest. The 2014 title will likely be the feather in his cap, but there was still drama lurking underneath the Argentine's jersey in the 2017 playoffs. Ginobili's clutch from-behind block on James Harden in the waning seconds of Game 6 in the second round sent the Spurs to the Western Conference finals. The guard played a valiant role in the subsequent series against Golden State, even starting Game 4 at age 39.

Like most of the Spurs, Ginobili's a truly unique player who bucked the trend, proving that south of the equator isn't just for soccer players. With career per-game averages of 13.6 points, 4 assists and 3.6 rebounds, 83 percent from the line and 37 percent from deep, the numbers don't tell the whole story for Ginobili, whom coach Gregg Popovich once said possesses a "maniacal approach to competitiveness." At times, there wasn't a man more important to his team, a glue guard who could play both positions and who accumulated four championship rings, two All-Star appearances and the everlasting respect of fans and players alike.

his point total to 20.8 points, proving he could play the game at an elite level and in crunch time.

His creativity with the ball is off the charts, from standard behind-the-back passes to between-the-opposing-legs-of-another-player-passes to laser passes off turnovers into the paint. Basically, Ginobili will make you shake your head at his creativity at least once a game.

In 2008 he was named Sixth Man of the Year, putting up 19.5 points per game

AL HORFORD 42

QUIETLY, ALMOST UNOBTRUSIVELY, Al Horford has become one of the best big men in the game, first helping propel the Atlanta Hawks from perennial first-round knockout to one of the premier teams in the Association, and now plying his trade for the legendary Boston Celtics organization.

Horford's quiet ascent may be because he hails from the Dominican Republic, a tiny island nation known primarily for producing baseball players. But Horford never picked up a glove. His father played pro basketball for several years, and with his son's height and interest in the game, the elder Horford moved the family to Michigan when Al was 14 years old. At the All-Star Game in 2015 Horford remarked, "I fell in love with [basketball] real quick, watching my dad play."

Horford set myriad high school records in his new home state before making the jump to college at the esteemed University of Florida. His move followed his father's footsteps, as Tito Horford went to the Sunshine State to suit up for the Miami Hurricanes in the late 1980s. The younger Horford made an immediate impact at Florida and, along with future NBA stars Corey Brewer and Joakim Noah, led the school during his sophomore year to an NCAA Final Four title against UCLA. It wouldn't be the last, as the trio tasted glory again the following year, and the center entered the NBA as a two-time national champion, something very few players can say.

Graceful even at 6-foot-10, Horford had a solid rookie year in 2007–08, putting up a respectable 10.1 points and 9.7 rebounds while averaging 31.4 minutes. He nearly duplicated those numbers the following year before breaking out in his third season in the NBA, with a per-game line of 14.2 points, 9.9 boards and 79 percent shooting from the line. More impressively, he's maintained a career .528 field goal percentage over the course of his 10 years in the league, dipping below 50 percent from the floor just twice.

Horford's an old-school center: a classic pick-and-roll big man who sets screens for guards like Isaiah Thomas to attack the basket or look for the open man. He's a strong presence on the back end and has been leader in Atlanta and Boston both on and off the court. He's also dialed in from the midrange, possessing a sweet stroke

defenders need to be wary of. He's a four-time NBA All-Star and now a fulcrum of the Celtics offense.

A torn pectoral muscle cost Horford more than half of his 2012–13 season, but in 2014–15 the Dominican essentially picked up where he left off and continued to cement his role on a pass-happy Atlanta offense that saw the Hawks post the second most assists per game (25.6) in the NBA.

Then-teammate Kyle Korver called Horford "the captain of our team" and "a calming presence." Maybe that's how Atlanta jumped out to a 35-8 start that season, putting together a 19-game winning streak and finishing 60-22 in the standings. In early 2015 Horford scored 19 points and plucked 16 off the glass against the Detroit Pistons. He dropped his first career triple-double against the Philadelphia 76ers three games later, recording 21 points, 10 rebounds and 10 assists during the Hawks' lengthy winning streak. Several days later he absolutely posterized Amir Johnson of the Toronto Raptors with a one-hand dunk after sidestepping Jonas Valanciunas. To cap off the month, he twice posted a double-double while adding three blocks. As this storied January 2015 shows, his smooth combination of skill, speed and athleticism makes him one of the most well rounded centers in the game.

Horford finished the 2014–15 season averaging 15.2 points and 7.2 rebounds per contest (and put up almost identical stats the following year). His consistency continued in the playoffs, and he helped the Hawks to the third round for the first time in 35 years.

After a disappointing second-round exit at the hands of the Cleveland Cavaliers in 2015–16, Horford elected to become a free agent. In 2016 he signed a four-year, $113 million contract with Boston, where alongside point guard Isaiah Thomas he helped lead the Celtics to the first spot in the Eastern Conference. In 2016–17 he averaged a steady 14 points, 6.8 boards and 5 assists a game, the latter a career high. He also hit a career-high 80 percent of his free throws in 2016–17.

Horford has fast become a household name, one of the greatest internationally born basketball players on the planet. And with his help, Boston appears to be a formidable threat to make deep playoff runs for years to come.

POSITION POWER FORWARD–CENTER / **SHOOTS** RIGHT / **HEIGHT** 6'10" / **WEIGHT** 235 LB. / **DRAFTED** 2008, SEATTLE SUPERSONICS, 24TH OVERALL

SERGE IBAKA [9]

THE FIRST NBA player from the Republic of Congo, Serge Ibaka rose to become the defensive force in the Oklahoma City Thunder's starting five before stops in Orlando and Toronto. And the 6-foot-10 power forward — who's a three-time All-Defensive First Team selection — is only getting better.

Ibaka may be Congolese, but he's multinational in terms of his citizenry. After cutting his teeth in the Spanish pro league, he loved the country so much he applied for citizenship. Once approved, he suited up for the Spanish national team, winning silver at the 2012 Olympics alongside the Gasol brothers.

Ibaka was selected by the Thunder (then the SuperSonics) with the 24th pick in the 2008 draft and debuted a year later as a 20-year-old in 2009–10. He saw limited action, suiting up for just over 18 minutes per game, and scored a respectable but unremarkable 6.3 points per game. His 5.4 rebounds per contest were stellar for his limited time on the floor, a strong indication of things to come. That season the Thunder managed to squeeze into the playoffs as the eighth seed, and while the veteran-laden Los Angeles Lakers eventually ousted the young team, Ibaka had time to shine.

The following season, Ibaka started 44 games, splitting duties with incumbent Nenad Krstic, and his numbers increased accordingly, with per-game averages of 9.9 points, 7.6 boards and 2.4 blocks. With the three-headed attack of Kevin Durant, Russell Westbrook and James Harden, the Thunder went deep into the postseason, losing in the third round to the Dallas Mavericks. The run established Oklahoma as a perennial playoff contender, and Ibaka, playing mostly center during his tenure in Oklahoma, proved to many that he was ready for the pressure of the big stage.

His arrival as a big-time defender came in his third season, 2011–12. Ibaka led all players in total blocks (241) and blocks per game (3.7) that season while adding a midrange jumper to his offensive arsenal.

CAREER HIGHLIGHTS

- Named to NBA All-Defensive First Team three times (2011–12 to 2013–14)
- Led the NBA in block percentage (9.8) in 2011–12
- Led the NBA in blocks twice (2011–12, 2012–13)
- Led the NBA in total blocks for four consecutive seasons (2010–11 to 2013–14)
- Won an Olympic silver medal with the Spanish men's basketball team in London in 2012

In 2012–13 his well-rounded play had him leading all NBA players who attempted 300 or more shots from the midrange in field goal percentage. His former coach, Scott Brooks, called Ibaka "one of the best midrange shooters in the league," and he was right, as his numbers bested All-Stars Chris Paul and Marc Gasol. His growing repertoire also spoke to the Congolese player's desire to get better in all facets of the game, and he didn't sacrifice his defense either, again leading the league in total blocks and blocks per game.

But 2014–15 was a difficult season for a Thunder team with championship aspirations.

Durant missed 55 games, Westbrook missed 15, Ibaka missed 18 and the Thunder missed the playoffs. Ibaka still finished third in the league in blocks per game with 2.4, and despite a dip in his typically stellar field goal percentage, his offensive numbers weren't far off pace given that Durant's absence often translated into fewer open looks for the big man. He finished the season with 14.3 points per game, 7.8 rebounds and a .836 free-throw percentage.

Ibaka bucked the trend of shot-blockers being simply that; he is now as well rounded a big as they come. "At that position, there are only a few guys that

can shoot that well," Westbrook said of his former teammate. In his final year in Oklahoma, Ibaka swatted away seven shots in a game versus Philadelphia, chipping in offensively with 11 points and 7 boards. Versus Golden State, he put up 15 points and hauled 20 balls off the glass. The team advanced to the Western Conference finals but fell to those same Warriors in seven games.

Soon after Ibaka was traded to Orlando, where he shifted between center and power forward to combat the trend of smaller opposing lineups that toss up more threes. Midway through the 2016–17 season he was moved again, this time to Toronto. He finished the season averaging 14.8 points and 6.8 rebounds and added a dangerous three-point shot to his arsenal. In the 2017 off-season, he agreed a three-year, $65 million deal to stay in Toronto.

Ibaka has put in a lot of hard work, which has brought him from war-torn Brazzaville to the Spanish league to the American Midwest and all the way to Canada. There, night in and night out, he sets up in the paint, patiently reading the post move of an opposing player, or he runs up the court, and instead of driving to the basket, he steps back, effortlessly for a big man, and hits nothing but net.

POSITION POWER FORWARD / **SHOOTS** RIGHT / **HEIGHT** 7'0" / **WEIGHT** 245 LB. / **DRAFTED** 1998, MILWAUKEE BUCKS, 9TH OVERALL

DIRK NOWITZKI 41

DIRK NOWITZKI IS a freak in the best way. Few NBA big men have been blessed with his rare combination of size and skill; fewer still come from Europe. Nowitzki grew up in Germany as an anomaly among anomalies. Born into an athletic family — his mother was a basketball player and his father played handball — Nowitzki even tried soccer and tennis before focusing on the rim. The decision paid off for the 7-foot power forward from Wurzburg, who has become the best European to ever play the game.

Rising above fellow big Hakeem Olajuwon on the NBA's all-time career points chart, Nowitzki cracked the top 10 in 2014 and made it to sixth of all time by 2016–17, cresting over LeBron James, the only other active player on the list. His point total is an impressive feat for anyone, let alone a Euro who was largely a mystery to anyone beyond the NBA's inner circle when he was drafted in 1998. Taken ninth by the Milwaukee Bucks, Nowitzki was traded on draft day to the Dallas Mavericks, where he has remained his entire career.

His rookie year was a challenging one as he adjusted to playing higher competition than in Europe. He averaged just over 20 minutes a game and collected 8.2 points and 3.4 rebounds as the Mavs finished well outside the playoffs. But an ownership change from Ross Perot Jr. to billionaire Mark Cuban altered the course of the franchise and Nowitzki's career as the Mavs went from a thrifty league also-ran

to a team that invested in success. Cuban upgraded everything: from the food the players ate and the hotels they stayed in to the arena they called home.

In Nowitzki's second season, the Mavs nearly made the playoffs and his numbers increased — 17.5 points per game, 6.5 rebounds and 2.5 assists. With a winning culture instilled in Dallas, the power

forward's third season was remarkable. The Mavs made the playoffs for the first time in over a decade, and Nowitzki significantly increased his output, putting up 21.8 points, 9.2 rebounds and 2.1 assists. He was finally adjusting to the bigger, faster forwards that had confounded him early on. That season "the Dunking Deutschman" also dropped more than 100 three-pointers and 100

blocks, becoming only the second NBA player at the time to do so and establishing himself as a threat to step back and knock down a deep ball. Although the Mavs bowed out in the second round to the San Antonio Spurs, the German forward impressed the league with a 42-point, 18-rebound performance in Game 5 of the series. That Mavs team also saw the emergence of another international star, Canadian Steve Nash, who arrived at the same time as Nowitzki (via trade from Phoenix), and the two formed a potent one-two punch for Dallas in the early 2000s. But in a tough conference, they made it no further than the Western Conference finals, and Nash returned to Phoenix.

Dallas eventually appeared in an NBA Finals, when Dirk powered the club forward in 2005–06, posting career-best totals of 26.6 points per game in the regular season and 27 points per playoff contest. Despite being up 2-0 over the Dwyane Wade–led Miami Heat, Dallas was torched in the next four, and Nowitzki's reputation took an undeserved hit as a choker.

Nowitzki set out to prove his detractors wrong the following year, winning the MVP award on 50.2 percent shooting and leading Dallas to a first overall regular-season finish in the West. But the team came crashing down again in the postseason, becoming the first number one seed to ever lose to an eighth seed. Again, in a league where only championships matter, Nowitzki was unfairly tagged as a player who couldn't get the job done when it mattered most.

Nowitzki is one of the few players in the league who can say he's played for just one team. And he is certainly beloved in Dallas. The 7-foot German has dominated in the post throughout his career thanks to a difficult-to-defend step-back jumper that's been his moneymaker during his 19 years in Texas. It was no more apparent than in 2011, when Dirk willed his way to a ring, as he and the Mavs defeated a Miami Heat team still trying to find its way after signing Chris Bosh and LeBron James. The win was extra sweet for Dallas, as the franchise was able to avenge its hard-to-swallow 2006 finals loss.

CAREER HIGHLIGHTS

- Named NBA Most Valuable Player for 2006–07
- Named MVP of the NBA Finals in 2011
- Won the NBA Three-Point Shootout in 2006
- Has played in 13 All-Star Games (2002–2012, 2014–2015)
- Averaged at least 21 points per game for 12 consecutive seasons (2000–01 to 2011–12)

Mavericks owner Mark Cuban has said publicly "he will never trade Dirk." The consummate professional, adored by his teammates, Nowitzki is a once-in-a-generation star, and in 2017 he hit the 30,000-point mark, just the sixth player to ever accomplish the feat. By the time he finally hangs them up, he'll surely go down as a Hall of Famer and the best foreign basketball player the NBA has ever seen. Until then, take joy in watching him step back in the paint, fall away and hit nothing but net.

SAN ANTONIO SPURS

POSITION POINT GUARD / **SHOOTS** RIGHT / **HEIGHT** 6'2" / **WEIGHT** 185 LB. / **DRAFTED** 2001, SAN ANTONIO SPURS, 28TH OVERALL

TONY PARKER ⁹

FEW EUROPEANS HAVE made as big an impact on the NBA as Tony Parker has in the last decade or so. The sly point guard, drafted 28th overall in 2001, has become one of the great international players of all time and one of the stalwarts on a San Antonio Spurs team that became a modern-day dynasty.

Scouted by then Spurs employee and current Oklahoma Thunder GM Sam Presti, the Spurs took a risk with Parker, an unheralded kid from across the pond who played one pro season in France and suited up internationally in FIBA's junior tournaments. Parker, whose mother is Dutch and father American, got his start

as a high schooler at INSEP, the top sports development program in Paris. Having never attended a U.S. college or played North American basketball, his first several years at the point running the Spurs' offense — with the likes of future Hall of Famers David Robinson and Tim Duncan — were challenging.

"It was hard the first three or four years," Parker recalled. Gregg Popovich, the Spurs' legendary coach, pushed the European to adapt to the NBA quickly, and it wasn't always pretty. "When I look back on it," Parker continued, "he made me very strong mentally."

Despite making 77 appearances his rookie year, he was still getting his sea legs in the NBA. Early knocks on Parker included questions about his physicality on the court, his lack of defensive prowess and his lackadaisical attitude in practice. His per-game line of 9.2 points and 4.3 assists was pedestrian, especially given his nearly 30 minutes of playing time.

His second season, 2002–03, saw a surge in production (15.5 points per game) that helped propel the Spurs to the 2003 championship. Excellent shot selection and strong dribble penetration are keys to his success on the hardcourt, and it was these elements that the future star began to hone.

After reworking his shot in the 2005 off-season, Parker turned a corner. With his new release, coupled with a renewed focus on taking two-pointers instead of three-

pointers, he shot above 50 percent for the first time in his career, posting a .548 field goal percentage. That mark remains his single-season high, and his career mark of .493 illustrates his continued commitment to wise shot selection.

Yet, like the best franchise players, he saves his best performances for the playoffs. When the Spurs swept LeBron James and the Cleveland Cavaliers in 2007, Parker was unstoppable, averaging 24.5 points per game and shooting 56.8 percent from the field en route to becoming the first European player to win the playoff MVP. "I'm speechless," he said after winning the award. "I put in a lot of work to get here." It was the third championship in five years and showed just how far Parker had come, from in over his head to hero in a matter of six seasons.

During the 2011–12 season, Parker set a career high in assists with 7.7 dimes per game to go with his 18.3 points over the course of the season. His role as ball

distributor and offense runner is a huge reason San Antonio has flourished all these years; his next-level basketball IQ is perhaps his most underrated quality.

Parker may be entering the twilight of his career, but he still makes an impact on the court, averaging 10.1 points and 4.5 assists in 63 starts in the 2016–17 season. It is certain Parker, Manu Ginobili and Duncan will go down as the greatest testament to international basketball in the history of the NBA. Together they were a nearly unstoppable force of nature, and despite their advancing ages still gave teams fits even as Duncan edged toward retirement at the end of 2016. Couple in their long relationship with coach Popovich, and it's clear that chemistry can mean everything to a basketball club.

The addition of LaMarcus Aldridge and the emergence of Kawhi Leonard as an MVP candidate have maintained the Spurs' status as a top team and given veterans like Parker and Ginobili a final kick at the can.

- Named MVP of the NBA Finals in 2007
- Named an NBA All-Rookie (First Team) in 2001–02
- Has played in six All-Star Games (2006–2007, 2009, 2012–2014)
- Is the all-time assists leader in San Antonio
- Is an eight-time NBA Player of the Week

Unfortunately, Parker suffered a season-ending quadriceps injury in the 2017 playoffs and was forced to the sidelines, a huge blow for a former NBA Finals MVP who until that point had played in 221 straight playoff games for the Spurs beginning in 2001.

With 16 seasons under his belt, Parker, a four-time NBA champion, will go down as not only the best French player in history but also one of the best international players the world has ever seen.

JONAS VALANCIUNAS 17

AS FAR AS international powerhouses go in basketball, Lithuania has always had a plethora of players who have made the jump to the NBA, especially centers. Names like Arvydas Sabonis and Zydrunas Ilgauskas paved the way for budding star Jonas Valanciunas, who is fast becoming one of the NBA's best young centers.

The young European comes from solid stock: his father was an elite rower and clearly passed along some genetic material perfectly suited for athletics. By 14, Valanciunas moved to the Lithuanian capital of Vilnius to take up basketball at a higher level, and he soon competed at the U16 European Championships as a 15-year-old. Selected fifth overall in 2011 by the Toronto Raptors, he debuted in 2012 with a solid line: 12 points and 10 rebounds in 23 minutes of action. Although he never jumped to the United States for college, the center hustled in Lithuania and briefly in the Euroleague before arriving in Canada, winning several gold medals at the FIBA tournament for his home country.

The scouting report on Valanciunas was that he was a determined youngster with a high compete level and a slick touch on the ball who was effective under the rim in catch-and-finish situations. That translated to ample time in a starting role for the then-lowly Raptors, as he registered 8.9 points per game, 6 boards and 1.3 blocks after starting 57 games as an NBA rookie.

Valanciunas has emerged as a bona fide weapon for the Raptors, who have now made the playoffs four straight years after a long period of watching from the outside in. At 7 feet tall and 255 pounds, he's a force in the paint, with nifty post moves that belie his size. Despite adding size since his rookie season, Valanciunas improved his footwork and regularly backs downs opponents, especially when his new brawn gives him a size advantage. One night in March of 2015, he deftly dropped a baby

Detroit Pistons in January. That spring, he kept it up, registering 26 and 10 against Cleveland in March when he went toe-to-toe with Timofey Mozgov, a fellow international baller and giant of a man who hails from nearby Russia. In the month of January alone, Valanciunas' field goal percentage was 61 percent, and he shot 87 percent from the line. In 2016–17 he recorded an 18-point, 23-rebound affair versus the Celtics in just 28 minutes of work. Two massive back-to-back stat lines in late March stood out as the Raptors marched toward the playoffs: 14 points and 15 rebounds versus Charlotte and 16 and 17 versus Indiana, with several key blocks. His coach Dwane Casey has praised his "skill, strength and willingness to work." Casey went on to laud how "coachable" the young Lithuanian is for the Raptors, especially in relation to those shrinking late-game minutes the center isn't quite ready for. Read between the lines and you get the idea Valanciunas is highly focused, patient with the growing process and looking to improve in all facets of the game. He was reduced to coming off the bench in the 2017 playoffs when opponents went small, which proves the Raptors center still has a ways to go.

Like many young players, he still has a lot to learn about getting quicker on the defensive end, but with his work ethic, Valanciunas should be poised in several years to be one of the best bigs in the league alongside LaMarcus Aldridge and DeMarcus Cousins, especially if he can add a three-point element to his game. The Raptors are hoping he evolves into a dependable double-double man, and the dream is that he consistently nets 20 points and 10 rebounds per game. In 2016–17 he averaged 12 points and 9.5 rebounds in 80 games of work and established career highs in points (32 versus Detroit) and rebounds (23 against Indiana). If Valanciunas can continue trending up, the Raptors have a star in the making, and he could quite easily surpass his forebears from his home country as one of the greatest basketball players to ever emerge from Lithuania.

CAREER HIGHLIGHTS

- Named an NBA All-Rookie (Second Team) in 2012–13
- Named Eastern Conference Rookie of the Month for March 2013
- Finished second in the NBA with a .572 field goal percentage in 2014–15
- Named FIBA World under-19 Championship MVP (2011)
- Named Lithuanian Player of the Year three times (2011, 2012, 2014)

hook on the legendary Tim Duncan. On other nights, he's running the screen and roll to perfection and barging his way to the basket. Is he a work in progress? Sure. But he's a near 80 percent free-throw shooter and averages just over 26 minutes per game.

He's come up huge in several games throughout his career. To start 2015, the Lithuanian put up 31 and 12 versus the

ORLANDO MAGIC

POSITION CENTER / **SHOOTS** RIGHT / **HEIGHT** 7'0" / **WEIGHT** 260 LB. / **DRAFTED** 2011, PHILADELPHIA 76ERS, 16TH OVERALL

NIK VUCEVIC⁹

FROM THE TINY country of Montenegro hails a giant. The son of Yugoslavian basketball players, Nik Vucevic followed in their footsteps, eventually landing in the United States with a thud, all 7 feet of him. He's become a quiet, unheralded star who might be the NBA's most under-the-radar center.

He spent three years with the University of Southern California Trojans after moving to the States and was drafted 16th overall in 2011 by the Philadelphia 76ers. But his stock truly rose after the draft when he spent time during the 2011 NBA lockout playing in Europe. Scouts marveled at his length, rebounding and creative scoring.

In his final year at USC, Vucevic managed 17.1 points per game and 10.3 off the boards before declaring for the draft following his junior year of college. He toiled for one year with the lowly Philadelphia franchise before a four-team, 12-player trade sent the European to the Orlando Magic, where he established himself as one of the most promising young big men in the NBA today.

When you're swapped in a deal that involves Dwight Howard, Andrew Bynum and Andre Iguodala, there's a lot to live up to. The weight was no problem for Vucevic. In January 2015, LA Clippers coach Doc Rivers called Vucevic "the best player in the league that nobody knows." Boston Celtics coach Brad Stevens went further, suggesting, "He may very well be an All-Star in the East at some point."

At 7 feet tall and 260 pounds, he's a quiet goliath, posting strong numbers in his sixth NBA season: 14.6 points a game and 10.4 boards. Coaches have admired his ability to shoot the basketball and handle the ball in the post. He may not be a block-happy center on defense, but he makes up for that at the other end, using both hands to make sly moves in the post, or popping off the pick and roll and making his way to the basket, preferring "short rolls, the half-hook or half-floater," as Vucevic put it midway through 2014–15. Plus, he has shown steady improvement — in year one with Philadelphia, he started just 15 games, played in 51 and averaged just 5.5 points and 4.8 boards. At the end of his fourth year (arguably his strongest season), Vucevic posted 19.3 points per game and 11 rebounds, and he put up a field goal percentage above .500.

In 2014–15, "Vooch" amassed 45 double-doubles, which ranked him fourth highest in the league behind DeAndre Jordan, DeMarcus Cousins and Andre Drummond. He posted back-to-back 30-point games,

and his best month of the season came in February: 22.2 points and 11.5 off the glass. He capped off the season with a 37-point, 17-rebound performance against the Minnesota Timberwolves on 18-of-25 shooting. In 2014 he signed a four-year, $53 million deal with the Magic, meaning Orlando fans won't need to worry about the center's future until 2018. He's enjoyed his time so much in Florida that he once claimed he wanted to be a member of the Magic for life.

The following year he averaged 18.2 points and 9 rebounds per game, recording a season-high 35 points versus Philadelphia in February 2016. During Orlando's 2016–17 season Vucevic once again averaged a double-double; however, his points per game average was down from 2015–16 and the Magic missed the playoffs. With a new GM, the European will be front and center as Orlando looks to turn things around.

Vucevic, alongside the Chicago Bulls' Nikola Mirotic and the Minnesota Timberwolves' big man Nikola Pekovic, is making a name for Montenegrin basket-

ball. Of the three Niks, it's Vucevic who could transform into a superstar. But the center from Montenegro will need to keep improving if he wants to lead the Magic back to the postseason and follow in the mammoth steps of another big who made a name for himself in Orlando, Hall of Famer Shaquille O'Neal.

CAREER HIGHLIGHTS

- Set a career high in points (37) in 2014–2015
- Finished second in two-point field goals (629) in 2014–2015
- Finished second in rebounding (11.9) in 2012–13 and sixth in rebounding (10.9) in 2014–2015
- Holds the Orlando Magic record for rebounds in one game (29)
- Drafted by the Philadelphia 76ers in the first round (16th overall) in 2011

CLUTCH PERFORMANCES

BASKETBALL IS REALLY quite simple. It's a quick, high-scoring game, with relentless up-and-down, back-and-forth action on the court. Twelve to a team. Five on the floor. Ten total. It's a sport played in two 24-minute halves and four 12-minute quarters. At times it's as complex as a high-screen pick and roll followed by a kick-out to the weak side for an open three, and sometimes it's simply one man versus another, mano a mano, with the clock winding down and nothing standing in the way but Father Time, a chance at immortality waiting.

Since James Naismith nailed two opposing peach baskets to the walls of a gymnasium in Springfield, Massachusetts, in 1891, the question of clutch has arisen in boardrooms and barrooms. Clutch is a measuring stick in the NBA by which men are judged and careers defined. In basketball, being clutch is everything.

There are clutch performers in every sport — the gunslinger QB in football, the shutdown goalie in hockey and the walk-off hitter in baseball. In basketball, clutch means a whole host of different things, but it is best encapsulated in one moment, one shot, one game, with everything on the line. Who emerges from the fray? Who, among the 10 men on the court, distinguishes himself in a league full of giants in a game that may be the last of the season? An athlete faces no greater test, no greater purpose, than rising to the challenge in the final minutes or seconds of a deciding game.

The Portland Trail Blazers' Damian Lillard, center, is mobbed by teammates after nailing a series-winning buzzer beater against the Houston Rockets in 2014.

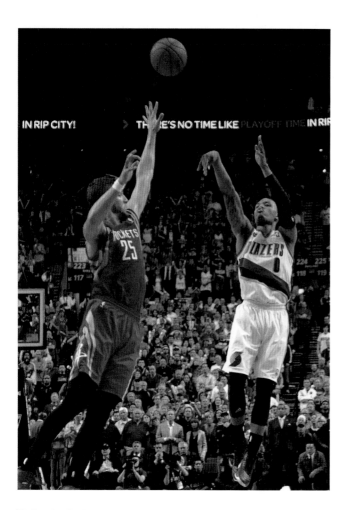

IN RIP CITY! > TH E'S NO TIME LIKE PLAYOFF TIME IN RIP

Portland's Damian Lillard watches his series-winning shot against the Houston Rockets' Chandler Parsons in 2014. The shot sent the Trail Blazers into the second round of the playoffs for the first time in 14 years.

Clutch also happens to be susceptible to the way we choose to remember things. With so many seasons, so many players and so many incredible moments, it's hard to recall what happened when. What year? What team? What shot? And even though memory-making moments now emerge more readily thanks to instant replay and 24/7 sports channels, the moments etched in NBA lore are the ones we choose to remember best. It could be the player, the circumstance or the feat itself — but like most things in life, not all clutch moments are created equal.

Take Michael Jordan's push-off, fadeaway dagger over Byron Russell to seal the 1998 finals, or Larry Bird's steal with seconds left in the 1987 Eastern Conference finals against Isiah Thomas and the Detroit Pistons that won the Celtics the game. Every market has a franchise-defining moment. For the championship-starved Portland Trail Blazers, Damian Lillard's series clincher on home court in the first round of the 2013–14 playoffs versus the Houston Rockets wasn't just a series winner. It was history for the fans in Portland.

But clutch moments also come in entire-game performances, not just instants in the waning moments of a game. Take Magic

Johnson's Game 6 performance in the 1980 finals, where the rookie point guard started at center in lieu of Kareem Abdul-Jabbar and casually contributed 42 points, 15 boards and 7 assists while going 14 for 14 from the line in 47 minutes. In 2012, ESPN ranked Magic's night number two all-time for single-game performances. And don't forget the legendary Bill Russell's ridiculous 10-0 record in Game 7s, capped off by a 30-point, 40-rebound performance in 1962. Michael Jordan was so clutch he didn't even need a Game 7 in any of the finals he played in. He claimed MVP of the NBA Finals six times — that's called rising to the occasion on the biggest stage possible, over and over again.

With the advance of analytics, the definition of clutch is being rewritten, and the new math is contributing in a macro sense to a better understanding of a player's worth on the court. Perhaps, though, it's reducing the way we approach the micro — there's still something magical about that game-winning shot or jaw-dropping jam, even if it's seen in a six-second video on our smartphones. There's still something powerful about watching greatness explode off the dribble, perfection rising off the floor and magic floating toward the basket in slow motion.

The thrill of witnessing "clutch" manifest is bigger than victory itself. It doesn't matter if you don't remember the details. You'll remember how it made you feel: one man, one bucket, nothing but net.

THE SHOT

Poor Craig Ehlo. His Cleveland Cavaliers were a rising power in the Eastern Conference and had drawn the Chicago Bulls in the first round of the 1989 playoffs. It was Jordan's fifth NBA season, and the Bulls had never advanced past the first round since he'd arrived. Cleveland had finished 6-0 versus the Bulls that year in the regular season, finishing third to Chicago's sixth place. Cleveland was the clear favorite and Jordan and the Bulls the underdog.

In the final game of the best-of-five first round, with three seconds left on the clock, Jordan pushed through the screen, grabbed the inbounds pass and made toward the top of the key, a half step ahead of Ehlo. People forget Jordan wasn't a game-ending legend until that bucket in Game 5. From 15 feet he rose up to shoot. Ehlo jumped and reached up and flew by as Jordan hovered a moment longer than Ehlo could hang with him, and Jordan hit the rising shot over Ehlo's disappearing fingers as the clock hit zero and the Bulls clinched the series. The lasting image of Jordan jumping into the air, pumping his fist and beating his chest, is as famous as the shot that inspired the celebration.

Ehlo became so defined by Jordan's moment that when the former Cavs forward recently entered a rehab facility for addiction to painkillers following back surgery, a kid recognized him as the guy who was guarding Jordan. Some nights, some plays, some games, good or bad, define you. They follow you everywhere. They become part of the larger basketball narrative. Ehlo's last words before the inbounds — "Mr. Jordan, I can't let you score" — add drama to the story. Poor Craig Ehlo.

Reggie Miller taunts New York Knicks celebrity fan Spike Lee after scoring 8 points in the final 18.7 seconds to steal Game 1 of the 1995 Eastern Conference semifinal.

It says something when one of the most clutch moments in NBA history involves two players. When a basketball play becomes known as "the Shot," something has captured the imagination of basketball fans. Jordan's make, even though it didn't lead to a title that year, became the emotional hump the Bulls franchise needed to become NBA champions in 1991. Maybe that is why the Shot etched its way into the global consciousness.

As far as buzzer-beating, series-ending shots go, it's hard not to put the Shot up there as one of the greatest of all time. The Bulls would go on to beat the Cavs five times over a seven-year span in the playoffs. LeBron James and company exacted some revenge in 2015 by slaying the Chicago dragon that has so often breathed fire on the Cleveland basketball community.

REGGIE AT MSG

Sometimes it's not a playoff winning shot, though. It's more than that. It's a deep rivalry that pits one man against an entire city. That man is Reggie Miller, and the city? Where else but New York.

On May 7, 1995, nine seconds felt like a lifetime for Knicks fans. It was the Indiana Pacers. Reggie again. Reggie at Madison Square Garden again. The same Reggie who put up 25 in the fourth quarter of Game 5 in the 1994 conference finals the year prior, a ridiculous performance that drew the ire of fans from across all five boroughs. The same Reggie who returned to MSG to exact revenge for losing that series and missing a chance to compete in the 1994 NBA Finals. And it would be the same Reggie who, in Game 1 of the 1995 Eastern Conference finals, put a dagger through the hearts of New Yorkers that night in May, in just nine seconds, cementing his ruthless, road-killer persona for years to come.

Few NBA players ignited a firestorm in a road building like Miller. Film director Spike Lee sat courtside and provided the perfect people's champ — a passionate celebrity fan with New York street cred who lived and died with the Knicks.

The back-and-forth trash talk between spectator and player was a legendary sideshow to the Indiana–New York rivalry, providing a perfect backdrop for "Miller Time." The Knicks, up by six with 18.7 seconds to go in Game 1, held a seemingly impossible lead. But Miller came down the floor and coolly knocked down a three to cut the lead in half. The guard then improbably stole the ball off the inbounds, and in a moment of complete cold-blooded hubris, he backpedaled behind the arc instead of going for the easy layup that would have cut the lead to one. He drained it, tying the game. The Knicks' John Starks then missed two free throws at the other end, and Miller came back down the court, was fouled and ended up at the line himself. In the span of nine seconds, the Knicks had gone from six points up to down by two, all in their home building at the hands of one man. Reggie.

As the buzzer sounded, Miller began mugging at Lee, grabbing his own neck. He yelled, "Choke artists!" while running into the tunnel following the robbery of Game 1, and the episode

became immortalized in the 30 for 30 documentary entitled *Winner Time*. Time and time again, Miller saved his best for MSG — countless playoff performances that stunned the crowd and cemented a lifelong beef with Lee. Six playoff series over a span of seven years will do that. But it was those eight points in nine seconds in Game 1 of the 1995 Eastern Conference finals that everyone remembers as one of the deadliest clutch performances in NBA history.

LARRY BIRD

But sometimes clutch isn't just one game. It's a career's worth of highlights that define a player's clutch-worthiness. One such man is "the Hick from French Lick," Larry Bird.

Legendary not only for his shot but also for his trash talk, Bird was unassailable. He once told Xavier McDaniel exactly where he would be on the court after a time-out before hitting the game-winner. One evening, he hit a game-winning shot with Jordan, no slouch on D, right in his face. Upon winning his third three-point shootout in a row at the NBA All-Star Game, Bird's iconic finger was raised in the air as soon as the ball left his hands — he knew he'd won in a moment reminiscent of Babe Ruth's called shot. And of course there was the steal, probably the most famous steal of all time, when Bird snatched Isiah Thomas' inbounds pass, fed the ball to Dennis Johnson and won Game 5 of the 1987 Eastern Conference finals with his defense. He didn't just want to beat you — he wanted to destroy you, squeeze you into submission, ensure you cried on your way home because you couldn't contend with greatness.

Bird may not have as many game-winners on the highlight reel as other players, but he was iconically clutch, winning three NBA championships in the 1980s — twice named the finals MVP, three times in a row the regular-season MVP. There was a stretch in the 80s when he was simply unstoppable. In 1984–85, Bird did it all: 28.7 points a game, 10.5 rebounds, 6.6 assists and .427 from three-point land. He was an 88 percent free-throw shooter, not even

his career high. In his third-last year at 34 years old, he shot 93 percent from the stripe, 21st all-time for one season, and he currently stands 11th all-time behind Reggie Miller. He didn't leave the league as a leader in any major categories, but his reputation was greater than that. Jordan, when asked once whom he'd pick to take the final shot, didn't hesitate: Larry Bird.

STEPH CURRY

If there's one player in the NBA currently holding the mantle for most clutch player in the league, it's not even close: Steph Curry. Yes, he's not yet 30. Yes, in recent years there have been more established superstars like Kobe and LeBron. But Kobe has retired and LeBron's catalog of buzzer beaters is thin, and a crop of young, big-time stars such as Curry is emerging around the league.

In his short tenure so far, Curry's past few seasons have proven

Stephen Curry, who scored 26 of his game-high 40 points after the start of the third quarter, celebrates Golden State's 123–119 overtime victory over the New Orleans Pelicans in Game 3 of their 2015 first-round series.

he's the purest shooter in the NBA, the biggest threat from behind the arc and perhaps the least clutch-looking guy on the court with that mouth guard wagging from his lips. He's not tall — 6-foot-3 on a good day — and he's slight. Not skinny necessarily, just slight-looking, a far cry from the trash-talking of Jordan and the mean-mugging of Bryant. He's a favorite of the analytics crowd, too. Curry plays admirable defense for an offensive threat and a smaller guard, ranking high in SportVU and real plus–minus, and he finished first in steals in 2015–16. He also shot 886 three-pointers, making 402, ranking him first with just over a .630 shooting percentage despite hucking up 200-plus more shots than his teammate Klay Thompson. He demolished Reggie Miller's playoff record of 58 threes by launching 98 over the course of the Warriors' championship run in 2015, and he is already in the top 10 all-time for most threes made. He set the record for most threes in one game — 13 — in 2016–17.

Curry's deadly in the final seconds of a game. In Game 3 of the first round of the 2014–15 playoffs versus the New Orleans Pelicans, the Warriors, up two games but down 20 on the road in the fourth quarter, mounted an unimaginable comeback, conducted by none other than their maestro, Curry, whose fallaway three with seconds left sent the game into overtime. It was on the Internet before he could peel his body off the court. Curry hit the final two free throws for 40 points total to secure the win. (He finished with 39 the next game as they swept the Pelicans.) It was symbolic of everything clutch — despite a cold start, he caught fire at the end of a playoff game, knocking down bucket after bucket until the ultimate shot. He would be named regular-season MVP days later.

Carmelo, Kobe, LeBron, even Durant — keep 'em — Curry is the guy down one, down three, down 20 who gets the ball.

THE AGE OF ANALYTICS

The definition of clutch shooting is going through a transitional phase as analytics become a source of information to fans and GMs in an attempt to gather the true value of a player to his team. Video cameras are ubiquitous devices in NBA arenas these days — SportVU cameras in the rafters, specifically, track every player's movement for the entire game. Sure, coaches still scratch Xs and Os on the sidelines during a time-out. But the real work is being done in dark rooms, far beyond the reaches of the court, where data gets sent from those cameras, which were installed at the beginning of the 2013–14 season. Statisticians and newly hired data analysts then review mountains of data. It's complicated stuff — most stats guys are professors or PhD students in economics and do not come from

Chris Paul steals the ball from LA's Nick Young in 2014–15. Paul led the NBA in steals that season; it was his sixth time leading the league in the stat.

sources of data so that we can improve performance of our players." Those PhD guys are even introducing papers that attempt to explain defensive worth on the basketball court, tracking and analyzing "counterpoints," which, according to now-shuttered Grantland, "estimate how many points an individual defender allows per 100 possessions."

In 2015 Alexander Franks and Andrew Miller, the authors of the study, suggested Chris Paul was the top defensive point guard in the league after crunching the numbers. Although it seems obvious to the naked eye that Paul is pretty money without the ball, the numbers backed it up, and we entered territory that the assistant vice president of Stats LLC called "the ability to measure the impact individual defenders are having throughout the game," a huge leap forward for the NBA. Paul's reputation as a winner had taken a hit over his career, thanks to few playoff series wins. That changed when Paul willed the Clippers past the reigning-champion San Antonio Spurs in a thrilling Game 7 victory in the first round of the 2015 playoffs, and his game-ending shot, off-balance with Tim Duncan's hand in his face, silenced his critics. The point is: it's easy to see Paul's worth when he nets a series winner. Those SportVU cameras recorded not only where Paul was on the court, and the two points that counted on the scoreboard, but also how he fared throughout the game. Beyond well-known players like Paul, general managers can use advanced statistics to identify undervalued players who add an element to the game beyond baskets.

a sports background. But they're massive basketball pioneers on the frontier of applying science to the hardcourt.

Shooting charts are growing in popularity and are easily available online. Phrases like "expected performance value," or EPV, are creeping into the casual fan's vocabulary, and stats like PER (player efficiency rating) and true shooting percentage are already mainstream on sites like basketball-reference.com. Adjusted plus–minus, or real plus–minus, is another stat gaining momentum on ESPN. In 2015 Dallas Mavericks owner Mark Cuban told ESPN that "Analytics have been an important part of who we are since I walked in the door 15 years ago. We have strived to introduce new and exclusive

Several GMs now come from an analytics background, including Houston Rockets head honcho Daryl Morey. The Rockets were the first team in the NBA to hire a cadre of stats guys in the front office to give them an edge. On the court, the team is led by James Harden, and the Rockets have all but eliminated a midrange jump shot from their offensive attack, taking an inordinate number of threes or shots in the paint not only because the stats back it up but also because the assembled personnel provide a reason to. If Harden or any of his backcourt counterparts miss one of their umpteen threes — they led the league in attempts in 2017 — the team is ready to gobble up the board by committee. In 2016–17 Houston finished in the top 10 for total rebounds without an elite rebounder.

Houston Rockets guard James Harden, the darling of the analytics movement, scores on a fast break layup against the Washington Wizards.

to understand a basketball player's worth, but it's growing in popularity. At the very least, for stats geeks around the world, it's provided an arsenal for debate at the bar when Harden pulls up for another three, or a lanky center settles for a long-range jack instead of attacking the rim.

The way we understand the game has certainly changed, and players like Harden and Russell Westbrook are being coveted in the draft. As a point guard coming out of college, Westbrook had his size and assist rate challenged. But Seattle/Oklahoma's brass saw an opportunity, and after his MVP-like season in 2014–15 and his assault on the record book in 2016–17, where he's carried the Thunder in every category, the Thunder management and their analytics team are looking like geniuses in identifying Westbrook's superstar talent.

There will always be obvious choices every draft. Andrew Wiggins and Jabari Parker were automatic top-two selections in the 2014 draft and immediate everyday NBA players. So were Karl-Anthony Towns and D'Angelo Russell, the number one and two overall selections in 2015. The trick is using analytics to go further. It's those teams at five through 10 who should be using everything available to make value judgments on future NBA players.

Not everyone, however, has embraced the new era of statistical data. In 2015 Charles Barkley called Morey "one of those idiots who believes in analytics." That season, the Lakers, Knicks and Nets had been well behind the eight ball in embracing the philosophy of numbers, and the Knicks and Lakers — unsurprisingly based on the advanced statistics — finished in the top five of field goal attempts made from 15 to 19 feet that year. In other words, they took a lot of poor probability midrange shots. The Rockets? They were dead last in this category.

So what does it say about the way we're understanding clutch? Maybe we're moving past the highlight-reel buzzer beater into the realm where a player's complete skill set comes into play over a longer period of time. Quantifying stats may not be the sexiest way

WE'VE COME A long way since Mr. Naismith, in that old gymnasium in 1891, recalled a game from his Canadian childhood named "Duck on a Rock" and went about creating the rules for a new game he'd call "Basket Ball." From no backboards and a closed hoop, we've arrived at a time and place that includes dozens of in-arena cameras, SportVU and the uber-analysis of the game at a second-by-second level. It's impossible to think what Naismith would have thought about all this technology. It doesn't mean that anything has irrevocably changed since Naismith wrote his first 13 rules — the game is fundamentally the same. There are still 10 men on the court, five a side, with the goal to put the ball in the opponent's basket. And what will never go away is that last-minute shot, the anticipation as the clock ticks down that one man is getting the ball and one man is defending him. One of them will walk off the court, head shaking. The other, arms raised, a hero.

KARL-ANTHONY TOWNS

POSITION POINT GUARD / **SHOOTS** RIGHT / **HEIGHT** 6'5" / **WEIGHT** 194 LB. / **DRAFTED** 2014, WASHINGTON WIZARDS, 46TH OVERALL.

JORDAN CLARKSON 6

IN A LOADED rookie class, Jordan Clarkson certainly felt under the radar to begin his first season, especially in the mentee role behind now-retired superstar Kobe Bryant. Clarkson thrived in 2014–15 for the rebuilding Los Angeles Lakers, and after three NBA seasons, he continues being the point man for a young team still in the midst of a rebuild.

Born to an American military father and Filipino mother, Clarkson is part of a new wave of players in the NBA that are adding to the growing mosaic of multiculturalism around the league. Raised in San Antonio, Texas, he played several seasons for the University of Tulsa before transferring to Missouri, where he showcased his skill set to NBA scouts, dropping 17.5 points per game in his final year of college ball. He even scalded powerhouse Kentucky for 28 points and appeared well on his way to a first-round selection in the 2014 NBA Draft. But after his father's cancer diagnosis, Clarkson's play dropped off, as did his hopes for an early draft spot. His father eventually recovered, and Clarkson was selected 46th overall by the Washington Wizards, who quickly traded him to the Lakers thanks to already owning a powerhouse backcourt in John Wall and Bradley Beal. The trade is now looking like an outright steal for the storied California franchise. The Lakers were looking to add a guard to complement seventh overall pick and power forward Julius Randle, who sat out 2014–15 with a knee injury suffered early in the season.

At 6-foot-5 and 194 pounds, Clarkson has a great blend of size and speed and can shift between both guard spots if needed. Clarkson possesses a strong rim attack, and his ball-handling skills — praised by everyone around him — are perfect for dishing on the slash or heading to the line for a few freebies. Carlos Boozer referred to Clarkson as "Baby Westbrook." He's also a highly motivated player: after a poor outing, he rewatched the NBA Draft multiple times to serve as inspiration for his next game. That act is either really badass or extremely masochistic.

If one good thing came out of the debacle that was Steve Nash's injury-riddled two seasons in LA, it's that the former two-time MVP was around to influence the Lakers' young core, including Clarkson, specifically offering him tips on creating space.

Clarkson started 38 games out of 59 during his rookie season, many of those during the second half with Bryant out. And he took full advantage of the opportunity, finishing February by averaging nearly 14 points, 4 dimes and a steal per contest, while shooting 85 percent from the line. Late in the season, he scored a career-high 30 points and added 7 assists to punctuate his coming-out party, following it up four games later with a fierce 26 points, 11 helpers and 6 boards against the Sixers, one of only two wins out of the last 10 for the Lakers as they finished out 2014–15.

And although he finished seventh in Rookie of the Year voting that year, he has become one to watch as the Lakers continue to retool the franchise and go young. His rookie totals (11.9 points, 3.5 assists, 3.2 rebounds, .448 field goal percentage) were all excellent signs that among a strong crop of first-year players, he was capable of playing at a high level night in and night out if given the opportunity. But that will be the question moving forward. Will the Lakers feel the need to improve at the point guard position by adding a veteran, or will they put their trust in Clarkson?

One writer called Clarkson "the lone bright spot" on an otherwise dismal team. The 2015–16 season was another challenging campaign for the Lakers, but highlights for Clarkson included a solid 25-point performance in the Rising Stars Challenge at the All-Star Game and a promising late-season game versus New Orleans where he drained 5 of 8 from downtown, 10 of 15 overall, and finished with 26 points. He finished the year averaging 15.5 points a game and established himself as a versatile point guard who can shift to the 2 spot if called upon.

Clarkson didn't start as many games in 2016–17 as in previous years, but he

came off the bench and averaged nearly 30 minutes a night and 15 points per game, including a 35-point effort against the Minnesota Timberwolves in which he notched 8 threes and a season-high 47 minutes.

Although he may not have been a high draft pick, Clarkson is proving his detractors wrong and remains an inexpensive option at point guard for the near future. His price, his attitude and, above all, his revelatory play have shown he may be a piece of the puzzle in Hollywood for a long, long time.

CAREER HIGHLIGHTS

- Named an NBA All-Rookie (First Team) in 2014–15
- Named Rookie of the Month for March 2015
- Finished second in rookie scoring (11.9) in 2014–15
- Finished third in rookie assists (3.5) in 2014–15
- Participated in the Rising Stars Challenge (2016)

DENVER NUGGETS

POSITION POWER FOWARD / **SHOOTS** RIGHT / **HEIGHT** 6'10" / **WEIGHT** 250 LB. / **DRAFTED** 2014, DENVER NUGGETS, 41ST OVERALL

NIKOLA JOKIC 15

NO ROOKIE FROM the 2015–16 NBA season made bigger strides than Serbian power forward Nikola Jokic, whose sophomore season caused a stir not only within the Denver Nuggets organization but all across the league. Known as "the Joker," the big man made such an impact offensively that he's become the central force in the Rocky Mountain state and the piece the franchise plans to build around for years to come.

Jokic finished third in rookie scoring in 2015–16, impressive for the 41st pick in

the 2014 draft. The 6-foot-10, 250-pound forward plays more like a guard. He has exceptionally soft hands and deft passing skills for a man who can easily shift between the 4 and the 5 positions on the court when called upon.

In February 2017, just days after Denver traded away fellow big Jusuf Nurkic, Jokic, with the frontcourt to himself, went off against the Golden State Warriors, dropping 17 points, 21 boards and 12 assists against a Golden State team that was coming off an emotional victory in Kevin Durant's first return to Oklahoma City. The Joker was grinning ear to ear. It was the first triple-double in NBA history with a shooting percentage of better than 50 percent. He then dropped an impressive 40 points at Madison Square Garden, which even on a good Sunday is a hostile environment for any visiting team. The Garden is still the biggest stage in basketball, even though the hometown Knicks are currently struggling. Those games opened everyone's eyes to the new face on the block.

To cap off that legendary February, the Serbian forward became the first Nuggets player to notch back-to-back triple-doubles since Dikembe Mutombo — first against Chicago, when he put up 19 points, 16 boards and 10 dimes, and then versus the Bucks, when Jokic notched 13 points, 14 boards and 10 assists. The following night, for good measure, he scaled Charlotte for 31 points on 13-of-15 shooting.

If he's not hitting shots, Jokic's a dish-first big. If the passing lanes are cut off, he drives to the basket with authority. His vision on the court is lauded. And he has gotten better at being a physical presence on the glass. He's a big who likes to dribble — he would have pretty much been a unicorn 10 years ago, but now, he's an extra threat for a team with strong outside shooting that includes up-and-coming Canadian Jamal Murray, the MVP of the Rising Stars Challenge at the 2017 All-Star Weekend. Although Jokic finished his rookie season with admirable stats in just 22 minutes per game — 10 points, 7 rebounds, 2.4 helpers, a decent 81 percent from the free-throw line and 33 percent from behind the arc — his numbers in 2016–17 have only gotten better, with him finishing at 16.8 points, 9.8 rebounds and 4.9 assists.

The Serbian is an interesting character — he misses the food from home so much he keeps a stash of Serbian meat in his freezer. As a kid, he was into offbeat sports such as harness racing and water polo. His heavily tattooed brothers, whom Jokic describes as "serial killers," are hardcore, vocal fans at Nuggets home games. And he's already picked up some international hardware — a silver at the U19 World Championship and a silver at the 2016 Olympics.

To say he's come of age quickly is an understatement. His meteoric rise in the second half of the 2016–17 season has been nothing short of amazing. He's prototypical of the new power forward in the NBA — both long and big, defensively responsible, strong under the rim and able to hit the occasional three. But what really separates him from the other power forwards is his vision on the court, as evidenced by his high assist rate. In 2016–17 he was in the top five among power forwards.

In the years to come, Jokic will likely shift between the 4 and the 5 spots, providing options for the coaching staff depending on the matchup. It won't matter whom he guards, though — he'll be a handful for bigger centers because of his sleek passing and ball-handling skills, and power forwards will struggle with his big body and deft post moves. For now, wherever he is on the court, Jokic makes his presence known. And if you're looking for a secret to the Serbian's success, just open his freezer.

CAREER HIGHLIGHTS

- Named an NBA All-Rookie (First Team) in 2015–16
- Finished third in NBA Rookie of the Year voting (2016)
- Finished fourth in triple-doubles (6) in 2016–17
- Won an Olympic silver medal with the Serbian men's basketball team in Rio in 2016
- Won a silver medal at the 2013 FIBA World U19 Championship

POSITION SHOOTING GUARD–POINT GUARD / **SHOOTS** RIGHT / **HEIGHT** 6'5" / **WEIGHT** 185 LB. / **DRAFTED** 2014, MINNESOTA TIMBERWOLVES, 13TH OVERALL

ZACH LAVINE 99

ZACH LAVINE IS dirty. As in dirty good. He may have gone unnoticed at the start of the 2014–15 season in his role as the Minnesota Timberwolves freshman not named Wiggins, but ever since his high-flying antics at both the 2015 and 2016 NBA All-Star Games, LaVine has proven he's one to watch.

At 6-foot-5 and 185 pounds, the shooting guard doesn't cut an imposing figure, but his talent level is off the charts. The Wolves needed athleticism — they'd yet to swing the deal with Cleveland for number one pick Andrew Wiggins following the 2014 draft — and coveted the UCLA product. What they got by selecting LaVine 13th overall was a multiposition guard who is proving he possesses a higher ceiling than people may have thought.

LaVine grew up in the Northwest, the son of a former football player. One of Washington State's best high school players, he jumped to the college scene, suiting up for the UCLA Bruins. He lasted only a year and wasn't even one of the best players on the team. But, boy, the kid could dunk (he sports a rumored one-step 46-inch vertical).

"Thank God for the Internet" must have been what every basketball fan muttered when LaVine showed up at the 2015 Slam Dunk Contest. Inside the Barclay's Center in Brooklyn, in the biggest city in North America, LaVine could not have picked a better or bigger arena to showcase his bag of tricks. Wearing the "Toon Squad" No. 23 jersey from the movie Space Jam — an homage to Michael Jordan — LaVine entered the arena to the theme song from the movie. It was nothing if not hubristic, but the kid from Washington walked the walk, demolishing the competition.

His first dunk: between the legs. His second: behind the back. Both spectacular. All four of his dunks were executed at a

CAREER HIGHLIGHTS

- Named an NBA All-Rookie (Second Team) in 2014–15
- Won the NBA Slam Dunk Contest twice (2015, 2016)
- Named Rising Stars Challenge MVP in 2016
- Finished second in rookie assists (3.6) in 2014–15
- Drafted by the Minnesota Timberwolves in the first round (13th overall) in 2014

high degree of difficulty, but most importantly LaVine had the crowd and a crew of NBA superstars on the sidelines jumping out of their seats. It was the most exciting dunk contest since Vince Carter brought the house down in 2000, and it has helped elevate LaVine's status around the league.

LaVine had many highlights that year outside the Slam Dunk Contest. In November 2014, he poured in 28 versus Kobe Bryant and the LA Lakers. Versus the Golden State Warriors, he racked up a

career-high 14 assists. In April 2015 — again against the top-seeded Warriors — LaVine saved his best for last, going off for 37 points, knocking down 6 of 10 threes on 13-of-21 shooting from the field, and adding 9 boards and 4 helpers. He finished his rookie season with 10.1 points, 3.6 assists and 2.8 rebounds, a solid contributor who was rewarded with increased playing time as the year went on. When point guard Ricky Rubio was lost to injury, LaVine gobbled up the minutes, playing out of his usual position but not looking out of position. He ranked second in rookie free-throw percentage, fifth in rookie scoring and eighth in rookie shooting percentage from behind the arc. Former coach Flip Saunders was impressed, stating at the end of the 2014–15 season, "Anytime . . . you can go through a stretch where you can play 10 games, [and] you can average 20 a game, that's impressive."

In 2015–16, LaVine continued to get better, playing all 82 games and averaging 14 points a contest. His 35 points off the bench — on 14-of-17 shooting, no less —

versus the Oklahoma City Thunder was an overture for the real symphony of the season: his head-to-head battle with Aaron Gordon in the 2016 Slam Dunk Contest. The competition required max effort from both the reigning champ and the eventual runner-up. With the crowd jumping out of their seats every time Gordon or LaVine threw it down — like LaVine's balletic flight to the hoop from just before the foul line — their performances were modern-day opuses for dunk enthusiasts.

LaVine started the 2016–17 season well, but an ACL injury landed him on the sidelines halfway through the campaign. But even before the season was out, his rehab was way ahead of schedule.

In June 2017, in a blockbuster draft-day deal, LaVine, Timberwolves teammate Kris Dunn and the 7th overall pick were traded to the Chicago Bulls for Jimmy Butler and the 16th pick. Chicago is looking to set a new direction for its team with this crop of young talent. Once healthy, LaVine will have the opportunity to define a new path for the storied Bulls franchise.

PORTLAND TRAIL BLAZERS

POSITION SHOOTING GUARD / **SHOOTS** RIGHT / **HEIGHT** 6'3" / **WEIGHT** 190 LB. / **DRAFTED** 2013, PORTLAND TRAIL BLAZERS, 10TH OVERALL

C.J. McCOLLUM[3]

C.J. McCOLLUM HAS finally arrived. The 6-foot-3 shooting guard was named the 2015–16 Most Improved Player, but he hasn't stopped there. The Portland shooting guard is one of the up-and-coming stars in the NBA. If 2015–16 was his breakout hit single, in 2016–17 McCollum stayed at the top of the charts.

It's always been an uphill battle for the once-diminutive Portland Trail Blazers shooting guard. It wasn't lack of talent but lack of size that held him back — McCollum stood just 5-foot-2 in his freshman year of high school. A late bloomer, he shot up in stature and played a starring role for Glen Oak High School in Canton, Ohio, once recording 54 points in a single game. "When you're smaller, you kind of learn how to do other things," McCollum said in 2013. "You have to work a little bit harder. Nothing really comes easy to you when you're under-recruited . . . undersized . . . undervalued. You have to be better than the bigger guys." McCollum was always in the gym, committed to getting bigger and stronger. His desire to win no matter what the cost was quickly evident; he even broke down crying one night on the floor during his first year of college, blaming himself for letting the older players down — something his coaches took as a sign of maturity. They knew they had a special player on their hands.

His passion paid off and McCollum proved his worth immediately, taking

CAREER HIGHLIGHTS

- Named NBA Most Improved Player for 2015–16
- Set a career high in points (43) in 2016–17
- Drafted by the Portland Trail Blazers in the first round (10th overall) in 2013
- Named Patriot League MVP in 2010 and 2012
- Is the Patriot League's all-time leading scorer (2010–13)

the relatively unknown Lehigh Mountain Hawks all the way to the 2010 NCAA tournament, where he stroked 26 points as a freshman in his first contest on the national stage. McCollum returned to the tournament two years later, knocking off second-seeded powerhouse Duke while leading the 15th-seeded Lehigh to a huge upset win. He stayed all four years at college, completing his journalism degree before being drafted 10th overall in the 2013 NBA Draft. Although McCollum didn't see regular minutes for several seasons in Portland, the talent and the

sweet stroke were there, and he went off for nearly 40 percent from behind the arc in his first two seasons.

His meteoric rise in the NBA coincided with receiving regular playing time, which shouldn't come as a surprise. But going from 6.8 points per game in his second season off the bench to over 20 a night as a starter in his third season — the largest increase for one player between seasons — caused quite a stir and led to his Most Improved Player award. In 11 games during the 2015–16 playoffs, he played more than 40 minutes a game, averaging over 20 points a night. He also provided fellow guard Damian Lillard with the backcourt help he'd long needed.

McCollum bettered his breakout campaign in 2016–17. In the first half of the season, he scalded the Pacers with 34 points, including seven threes. On New Year's Day, he dropped 43 points — a career high — versus Minnesota. In McCollum and Lillard the Blazers have

one of the best guard combos in the NBA. McCollum's three-point shooting is getting even better, and his free-throw shooting was flirting with 90 percent all 2016–17. But more important, No. 3 looks as if he belongs with the top shooters in the game, and he's also under contract until 2021, something Trail Blazers fans should be thrilled about.

It's not all rosy though. McCollum needs to work on getting his assists and rebounds totals up — under four per game won't cut it in superstar land — but because his lights-out shooting keeps contributing to wins and playoff appearances, there's plenty of time to develop a full arsenal in the coming years.

Portland is still a ways away from moving up in the tough Western Conference, but clearly with LaMarcus Aldridge's departure in 2015, the torch has been passed to the backcourt. Rip City has a new lieutenant in C.J. McCollum, and it's time to salute one of the NBA's rising stars.

POSITION POWER FORWARD / **SHOOTS** RIGHT / **HEIGHT** 6'11" / **WEIGHT** 228 LB. / **DRAFTED** 2013, NEW ORLEANS PELICANS, 6TH OVERALL

NERLENS NOEL ③

THERE WEREN'T A lot of bright spots in the 2014–15 season for the Philadelphia 76ers. They came out of the gate with a 17-game losing streak and appeared headed for one of the worst seasons in NBA history. But one man stood out on this lackluster squad, easily identifiable by his distinct haircuts. Nerlens Noel, at 6-foot-11 and 228 pounds, seemed poised to lead this franchise out of the darkness and into the Promised Land, but instead a mid season trade in 2016–17 to the Dallas Mavericks has given Noel a new lease on life.

The son of hardworking Haitian immigrants, Noel was a massive prospect in the Boston area at Everett High before he even set foot on a college court. In 2012, his high school senior year, he was named top player in the USA, and he finished his senior season on scholarship with the prestigious Tilton School in New Hampshire after being heavily recruited away from his hometown. Before he'd even reached the NBA, the *New York Times* hailed him as "the best shot-blocker of his generation."

Playing nearly his entire rookie season, and starting most games, it was a trial by fire for the 22-year-old from Massachusetts. He suited up just one year for the storied Kentucky program before he was drafted sixth overall by the New Orleans Pelicans in 2013. Following the draft, he was traded to the Sixers for Jrue Holiday. But he missed a year after tearing his ACL and didn't dress until 2014–15. His numbers at Kentucky were impressive though — 10.5 points, 9.5 rebounds and an unreal 4.4 blocks.

Noel finished his rookie season averaging 9.9 points and 8.1 rebounds to go along with a solid 1.9 blocks per game, eighth in the league. It was an impressive showing for a freshman, especially one who missed an entire season of basketball. In addition, his 1.8 steals is incredible for a big man, and he finished with more than 100 blocks and 100 steals, a rare feat achieved in the NBA. His massive 7-foot-4 wingspan, quickness and leaping ability cause havoc for opposing teams, and the league is finally seeing the attributes Noel carried with him throughout high school and college. Comparisons to Patrick Ewing, David Robinson and Hakeem Olajuwon have followed him, and it's showing.

In February of his rookie year he was a beast, recording 12 points, 9 boards and 9 blocks against the Indiana Pacers, just missing the elusive blocks-inclusive triple-double. By March, Noel had rounded into form, averaging 14.3 points per game and 11.2 rebounds during the month. In his most productive offensive game that season against the Los Angeles Clippers,

- Named an NBA All-Rookie (First Team) in 2014–15
- Finished eighth in blocks per game (1.9) and total blocks (142) in 2014–15
- Led all rookies in rebounding (8.1) in 2014–15
- Finished sixth in rookie scoring (9.9) in 2014–15
- Drafted by the New Orleans Pelicans in the first round (6th overall) in 2013

and haircut — which has its own Twitter account — are trending positive. The following season he averaged 11.1 points, 8.1 rebounds, 1.5 blocks and 1.8 steals, punctuated by a 24-point game on 10-of-15 shooting versus the New Orleans Pelicans, and 14 points, 16 rebounds and an insane 7 steals late in the season against the Washington Wizards. Despite their rising star's personal growth, the 76ers continued losing.

In 2016–17 Noel began the season on the injured list and never found his rhythm. The Sixers brass opted to trade him to the Dallas Mavericks at the trade deadline for a couple of bodies and draft picks. With a glut of talented high-end forwards and centers in Philadelphia — Jahlil Okafor, Joel Embiid and the incoming first overall pick Ben Simmons — the logjam up front was getting real. In the fourth game with his new club, Noel hauled down 17 boards, a season high. His defensive prowess should be a nice transition out of the era of Dirk Nowitzki, an automatic Hall of Famer who is slowly riding off into the Texas sunset. In a couple of years we may look back at this move as the beginning of something truly special in the Lone Star State, with Noel potentially inheriting the man-in-the-middle title in Dallas for years to come.

he went for 30 points and 14 off the glass on 12-of-17 shooting, big numbers for Philly's rookie. Most impressive? On March 20, he became the youngest player in NBA history to record 20 points, 10 rebounds, 5 steals and 3 blocks in a game.

And although he wasn't Rookie of the Year — he finished third — he certainly turned heads, particularly late in the season, making voters take notice that it wasn't a one-horse race with Andrew Wiggins in pole position. He led all first-year players in rebounds, blocks and steals and began showing signs of becoming a truly unique talent, more like a Joakim Noah than Ewing.

The Sixers lost their last 10 games in 2014–15, and coupled with that early 17-game losing streak, the experience was tough on a talent like Noel. But his attitude

PHILADELPHIA 76ERS

POSITION CENTER / **SHOOTS** RIGHT / **HEIGHT** 6'11" / **WEIGHT** 275 LB. / **DRAFTED** 2015, PHILADELPHIA 76ERS, 3RD OVERALL

JAHLIL OKAFOR 8

WHEN 6-FOOT-5 JAHLIL Okafor entered his freshman year of high school, there was little doubt what path the future NBA star was walking down. Growing up in Chicago, Okafor played against Jabari Parker, another local star and future NBA player, and followed in the footsteps of Chicago natives Derrick Rose and Dwyane Wade, both decorated MVPs. Now Okafor's the latest Chicago basketball prodigy to hit the NBA, and the prospects are looking bright for the Windy City center.

Okafor spent just one year at Duke, but his numbers during that freshman year were astounding — 17.3 points and 8.5 rebounds. With Okafor down the middle, the Blue Devils captured the 2015 NCAA title, and the spotlight never left the big man. A dominant rookie throughout the year, he won multiple awards and posted serious individual numbers, including 30 points versus Virginia Tech and a college-best 25 and 20 game versus Elon University.

There was no doubt he was NBA-ready. Months after his college title, Okafor was drafted third overall by the Philadelphia 76ers.

Okafor's rookie season in 2015–16 was by all means a success despite the 76ers' struggles. A minor knee injury kept him out for most of the second half of the season, but he still managed to average 17.5 points and 7 rebounds per game in 30 minutes of court time. Establishing his monstrous 6-foot-11 and 275-pound frame

in the paint, he proved he could be a force once he polished his post game.

His second season in the NBA was impressive at times, and the 76ers improved after several years occupying the NBA's basement. Okafor dropped 26 points in

mid-January versus the Wizards, and despite suffering a few bumps and bruises, he seemed capable of holding down the fort in the middle. That gave Philadelphia options — with the emergence of another pure center, Joel Embiid, as a bona fide star and

- Named an NBA All-Rookie (First Team) in 2015–16
- Drafted by the Philadelphia 76ers in the first round (3rd overall) in 2015
- Won the NCAA Championship (2015)
- Awarded co-MVP at the McDonald's All-American Game (2014)
- Won a gold medal at the 2013 FIBA World U19 Championship

the trade of forward Nerlens Noel to Dallas, the floor space opened up for Okafor to shift to power forward if need be to accommodate Embiid's presence. With 2016 number one overall pick Ben Simmons finally set to start in 2017–18 (he spent his entire first season injured) things are looking up in the City of Brotherly Love. But it will be a work in progress to accommodate all three bigs, each of whom is looking to make a Rocky-like impact on Philly fans.

Okafor's had his share of missteps — during his rookie season, cameras caught him in a physical altercation outside a nightclub. And while his numbers haven't hit superstar status quite yet, he's still very young and barely out of his second NBA season. But like Philadelphia's patron sports saint, Rocky Balboa, whose statue stands northeast of "the Rocky Steps" outside the Philadelphia Museum of Art, Okafor needs to dig deep if he wants to come out on top.

From the beginning, it hasn't been an easy journey for Okafor. His mother, a great baller in her own right, passed away when he was just 9 years old. From his mother's home in Oklahoma, Okafor moved in permanently with his father in Chicago, where he and his dad turned this tragedy into a positive, motivating force that would fuel Okafor's game. His father, a former college basketball player, dedicated himself to coaching his son and preparing him to be an NBA star. It worked, and the father–son duo has been an inspiration around the league.

The next step is for Okafor to adapt to a new role with the 76ers: a player who can share the floor with other bigs and not be the center of attention on the court like he was at Duke. Rumors abounded that he was on the move at the 2017 trade deadline, but for the time being, he's in Philadelphia. Okafor can have nights where he drops 28 points and hauls down 10 boards on 11 of 19 shooting, as he did in the tough one-point loss to the New York Knicks in late-February 2017. With those kinds of numbers for such a young player, it's safe to say the best of Okafor is yet to come.

KRISTAPS PORZINGIS 6

THERE WAS ONE bright light in an otherwise dim 2016–17 season for the once-storied New York Knicks, a team that failed to make the postseason and continues its free fall from flagship franchise in the 1990s to current NBA whipping post. That bright light is hard to miss — a 7-foot-3 Latvian named Kristaps Porzingis, who may be the only hope left for New Yorkers.

The lanky power forward had an unusual journey to the NBA, skipping U.S. colleges and suiting up for CB Sevilla in the Spanish League as a teenager. He plugged away for several years in Spain, honing his game and getting bigger and stronger. Despite being eligible for the draft in 2014, Porzingis waited one more year to fill out. It paid off, and he was named the EuroCup Rising Star in 2015.

His tenure with the Knicks didn't begin well. Porzingis was widely booed on draft day by Knicks fans unfamiliar with the European. They thought they were getting another Euro big who would eventually become a bust, but those naysayers will be eating humble pie for years to come because the Latvian's skill set is one of a kind. Porzingis possesses guard quickness in a center's body, a willingness to take abuse under the rim and a dazzling array of ball skills. The fourth overall pick made an immediate impact in the NBA, ending his rookie season with 14.3 points per game, 7.3 rebounds and 1.9 blocks and giving Knicks fans a dash of hope.

Those hopes were shattered as the 2016–17 season began falling apart for the Knicks: newly acquired point guard and former MVP Derrick Rose abruptly left the team before a home game to attend to a family matter back in Chicago, and

Carmelo Anthony found himself in a Twitter war with former Knicks executive and Chicago Bulls mastermind Phil Jackson about the direction of the franchise. Trade rumors also dogged Melo as the team lost game after game to start 2017, limping into

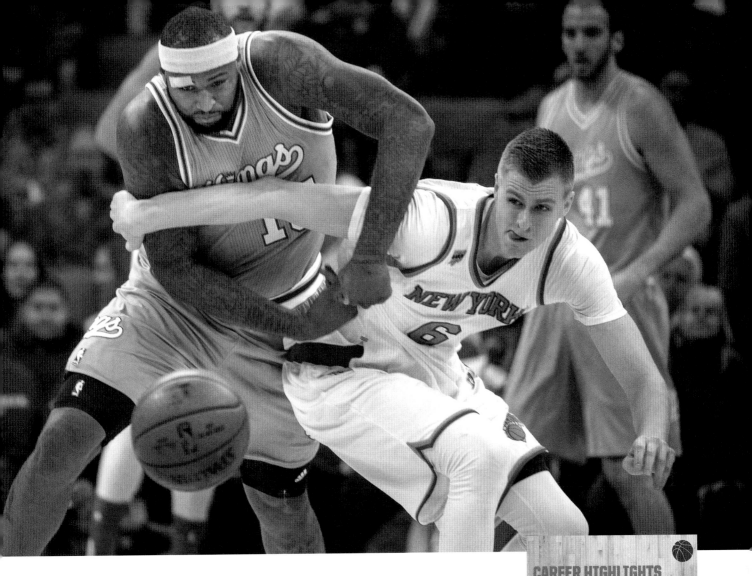

the All-Star break with a 23-34 record. The tipping point arrived when Knicks legend Charles Oakley was arrested in the stands and thrown out of the arena on trumped-up charges that included disturbing the peace and trespassing. (Porzingis was quietly shooting free throws when the melee began.) This was all before the 2017 All-Star break, and the season shaped up to be a far cry from the 1990s when Oakley and Patrick Ewing were leading the Knicks deep into the playoffs year after year.

Unlike his team, "Porzingod" smartly avoided any controversy during his second NBA season. (Being hurt may also have helped him stay out of the media's lens.) He finally figured out New York City, too. "I was getting caught up in traffic all the time," he joked in early 2017.

For a big man, there's few like him. With unnatural length and a 240-pound frame, Porzingis is a force in the post. But his perimeter game and behind-the-arc antics are unlike those of anyone his size. When he puts the two skill sets together, there's no stopping the Knicks power forward, and he explodes on the court. His sophomore numbers have been solid — with increased minutes he shot the ball better from behind the three-point line and played a more important role in the Knicks offense. In December against the LA Lakers, he dropped 26 points, 13 boards and 7 blocks. The following night he lit up the Phoenix Suns for 34, going 4 for 4 from deep. Injuries in January hampered Porzingis, but he finished strong once the drama in New York subsided. He also won the Skills Challenge at the All-Star break against some very talented guards, showcasing just how good he is for a man his size.

He may quickly become the focal point of a Knicks rebuild — a lot of pressure to put on a young man's shoulders. But he's refreshingly mature, spends most of his time with his family (who moved to

- Named an NBA All-Rookie (First Team) in 2015–16
- Won the All-Star Game Skills Challenge in 2017
- Finished second in Rookie of the Year voting in 2015–16
- Is a three-time NBA Rookie of the Month
- Named EuroCup Rising Star in 2015

New York when Porzingis was drafted) and finally understands the rigors of an 82-game schedule. The thing standing in his way might not be the opponents on the other side of the court, but the men pulling the strings up in the fancy suites at Madison Square Garden. The current Knicks franchise may be a gong show, but at least they got one thing right when they selected Porzingis.

MINNESOTA TIMBERWOLVES

POSITION CENTER / **SHOOTS** RIGHT / **HEIGHT** 7'0" / **WEIGHT** 244 LB. / **DRAFTED** 2015, MINNESOTA TIMBERWOLVES, 1ST OVERALL

KARL-ANTHONY TOWNS 32

TO SAY KARL-ANTHONY Towns has arrived is sort of like saying the Earth is round. No rookie made more of an impact on the NBA in 2015–16. Now, after concluding his sophomore campaign, the 7-foot center has already proven to Minnesota Timberwolves brass and players around the league that he is no flash in the pan.

His rookie numbers were nothing short of spectacular — 18.3 points, 10.5 rebounds, 2 assists and 1.7 blocks per game. Towns took home the hardware for Rookie of the Year, which meant the T-Wolves captured back-to-back rookie trophies, with Andrew Wiggins winning the 2014–15 honor. The decorated rookies have formed the

cornerstones of the Timberwolves team. When former guard Zach LaVine suffered a torn ACL at the beginning of 2017, many turned to Towns as the player to carry the torch. Unfortunately it was another losing season for the young squad.

Towns was born in Piscataway, New Jersey, a phenom since birth. Literally. He was featured on a television news broadcast as a newborn in 1995 because of his extreme size — 10 pounds and 25 inches long, bigger than every other baby photographed that day. His parents scraped away to buy him a hoop and build a court on their property, and by the time he reached high school age, he was a dominant force against older boys and near perfect academically. Yet all the attention never seemed to fluster the even-keeled but ultra-competitive center. Instead, he channeled his energy into becoming the best player he could.

At 16 years old, Towns suited up for the national team of the Dominican Republic (his mother's home country) and played under University of Kentucky's legendary John Calipari, forming a relationship that continued when Towns attended Kentucky. Standing then at 6-foot-10, he'd already won a high school state title in New Jersey. Towns continued raking against older players before finally declaring his intent to play ball in the storied Kentucky program. He flourished in his only college year, averaging 10.3 points per game in just 21 minutes a night. He played alongside future

- Named NBA Rookie of the Year for 2015–16
- Won the All-Star Game Skills Challenge in 2016
- Named Western Conference Player of the Week for March 2017
- Finished second in double-doubles (62) in 2016–17
- Finished sixth in rebounding (12.3) in 2016–17

February. He's an automatic double-double every night and someone who can carry the Wolves when the guards go cold.

More important, his willingness to learn and get better is off the charts. He lapped up every drop of knowledge mentor and retired veteran Kevin Garnett offered. Towns' father said, "The best thing to ever happen to Karl is Garnett." Garnett displayed legendary intensity, refusing to miss practice, arriving early and staying late, talking to himself. Towns also calls on an imaginary friend named Karlito to fire himself up. "You can't teach the beast," Garnett said early in Towns' rookie season, referring to his energy level. "You can't go to the store and buy a six-pack of beast."

Not many people can handle Garnett — learning from such an intense veteran competitor reveals what drives Towns beyond basketball. That drive is a quality teams hope for when they draft a kid first overall; they want a player with that intangible winning spirit found in so few NBA players. It's practically unteachable. Towns appears to possess it in spades.

A perfect blend of intelligence, ambition, talent and will, Towns has been given the tools by numerous mentors and handed the keys to the franchise. Now it's time for the young phenom to grow into the man. At 7 feet and 244 pounds, he's well on his way.

NBA players Devin Booker and Willie Cauley-Stein, and the young team made it all the way to the Final Four. Towns didn't stay long at Kentucky despite his commendable 3.6 GPA. After entering the 2015 NBA Draft, he landed in Minnesota as their number one pick.

Towns has fast become one of the most complete big men on the hardcourt. He posts up, steps back, spins, runs the court, plays D — the list goes on. The crazy thing? He improved in nearly every offensive category in the 2016–17 season. Plus he's capable of making opponents look silly anytime, anywhere. Take the 41 points and 16 rebounds he put up versus Houston just before Christmas, the triple-double a week later in Denver (15 points, 11 boards and 10 dimes) or the 37 points and career-high 22 rebounds against Houston in late

MINNESOTA TIMBERWOLVES

POSITION SHOOTING GUARD / **SHOOTS** RIGHT / **HEIGHT** 6'8" / **WEIGHT** 199 LB. / **DRAFTED** 2014, CLEVELAND CAVALIERS, 1ST OVERALL

ANDREW WIGGINS 22

NOT MANY NBA rookies have had to deal with as much fame as Canadian Andrew Wiggins. The first overall pick of the 2014 draft has handled the circus with aplomb and grace, qualities sure to be fundamental as he embarks on a long career in the NBA.

Hailing from Toronto, Ontario, the new hotbed of international basketball thanks in part to the success of Vince Carter a decade ago, Wiggins was a rising star as a teenager and was quickly noticed by pundits down south. Like other Canadians before him, he jumped ship for the opportunity to play for the prestigious Huntington Prep High School in West Virginia, an incubator for future NBA talent.

Following his senior year at Huntington, Wiggins shipped off to the University of Kansas for a classic one-and-done experience: promising NBA first-rounders choose schools that will hone their skills for just one year before declaring eligibility. It paid off. All freshman year, Wiggins, under the tutelage of coach Bill Self, was the talk of the NCAA. In 35 games with the Jayhawks, Wiggins averaged a team-high 17.1 points per game, as well as 5.9 rebounds and 1.5 assists. Although the numbers weren't eye-popping across the nation, the fact Wiggins had just turned 19 fueled speculations he'd go first or second overall. Possessing raw athleticism, smooth jumping ability, sound defensive awareness and an otherworldly vertical of 44 inches (among the highest ever recorded), Wiggins was too skilled

CAREER HIGHLIGHTS

- Named NBA Rookie of the Year for 2014–15
- Named an NBA All-Rookie (First Team) in 2014–15
- Named Rookie of the Month four times in 2014–15
- Is only the second Canadian to be selected first overall in the NBA draft
- Named Gatorade National Player of the Year in 2013

to let drop to second, and he was drafted by the Cleveland Cavaliers first overall. It appeared Wiggins would play student under the mentorship of LeBron James — a Cavalier again after his triumphant announcement that he was leaving the shores of Miami for his hometown, where he began his career. But the celebration for Wiggins would be short-lived.

Rumors abounded the Cavs were looking for another piece to their push for a championship — the Minnesota Timberwolves' Kevin Love. Wiggins, however, had signed with the Cavs and could not be traded for a 30-day period owing to a clause in the collective bargaining agreement. Thus, the 19-year-old remained in limbo, a sitting duck until the deal could be formalized. In late August 2014, Wiggins became only the second number one draft choice since 1976 to never play for the team that drafted him when Cleveland sent Wiggins and fellow Canadian Anthony Bennett to Minnesota for Kevin Love.

When the T-Wolves finally introduced Wiggins to the public, he was all smiles. "It's been a crazy summer," he said in August 2014. "But I wanted to play for a team that wanted me." The two Canucks form a formidable one-two north-of-the-border punch for the Minnesota fan base,

which should suit them both fine, since Minneapolis is the chilliest city in the NBA (not Toronto, despite the popular "We The North" campaign). As Wiggins told his former Jayhawks coach Bill Self at the time, "It's better for me . . . to go somewhere where I'm forced to be something."

It might take a few more years for Wiggins to become a bona fide superstar, but he's getting there after three seasons in the NBA. His first game for Minnesota was largely forgettable (6 points in 19 minutes of play), but he improved throughout the year, recording his first double-double in early December (23 points and 10 assists) in an upset win over the Portland Trail Blazers. On his 20th birthday in late February 2015, he scored 30 points and added 6 boards, proving he possesses the panache to be dominant in the league. Wiggins became the first Timberwolves player to win Rookie of the Year, finishing with 16.9 points and 4.6 rebounds per game.

Despite a losing season in his first year with Minnesota — the team had the worst record in the league — Wiggins proved he could be a go-to option from the perimeter and a basket-attacking force on one end, as well as a defensive stalwart on the other thanks to his enormous wingspan. In his second year, the shooting guard scored 32

points, 10 boards and 6 assists against the Sacramento Kings in December, joining an elite company — with members like LeBron James and Kevin Durant — of 20-and-under superstars who can put up that kind of stat line. In 2016–17, he averaged 23 points a night while playing over 37 minutes a game, the latter good for third in the league. He showed flashes of brilliance throughout the season, including a career-high 47-point night in November 2016 versus the LA Lakers and back-to-back 40-point affairs late in the season.

Get used to seeing Wiggins and the T-Wolves becoming a dominant presence. With Karl-Anthony Towns, another first overall pick, emerging as a potential superstar and former Bulls forward Jimmy Butler joining the squad in the 2017 off-season, Minnesota will be a team to watch in the coming years.

THE PLAYOFFS

THE REGULAR SEASON is like a warm-up jacket or a practice jersey, an opening act if you will. Most of the work is done in the lengthy grind, and it does separate the real athletes from the pretenders, but postseason performances are where careers are forged and reputations made. Regardless of regular-season numbers or record-setting seasons, it's rings that matter, not points per game. Whether that's fair or not is another conversation entirely. But in basketball, what separates the good from the great is your ability to come through when it truly matters.

Like the clutch performance conversation, the debate never ceases to double-back on the same questions. Who was the greatest of all time when it mattered most? Who stepped up at a crucial moment? Immortality and everlasting fame, in the annals of sport, art and war, have always been more interesting than one brief moment of glory. Since the days of gladiator pits, the Trojan War and the sacking of cities, having one's name written down in the record books is what lifts men from mere mortals to gods. Modern times are no different, and in the sport of basketball, the playoffs are king. So what better way to start than with the reigning monarch of the court?

The Cleveland Cavaliers' LeBron James answers questions at a press conference following Game 7 of the 2016 NBA Finals. The Cavs defeated the Golden State Warriors to claim Cleveland's first-ever NBA championship.

KING JAMES VERSUS MICHAEL JORDAN

LeBron James — LeBron — the single-name, one-man highlight reel, has succeeded so thoroughly that fans don't even notice how easy he makes it look. A lightning rod for praise and criticism, James has now appeared in seven straight finals from 2011 to 2017, the first to do so since Bill Russell made 10 straight from 1957 to 1966. He's won the regular-season MVP award four times, so we know how good a player he is on the march to glory. But what about the finish? With three wins and five losses in eight trips, he's been, well, middle of the road with respect to those rings. And of course, it wasn't without controversy that he and Chris Bosh flipped the tables on free agency and agreed to sign with the Miami Heat to join friend and All-Star Dwyane Wade. Manufactured? Sure. But that doesn't dismiss the fact that LeBron led the Heat through four straight seasons and four straight postseasons. That's a lot of wear and tear and playing consistently at a high level, so no wonder he was banged up early in 2014. But as he continues through his thirties, the discussion has focused less on his choices and more on his legacy, specifically related to Michael Jordan.

LeBron will always be compared with Jordan, no matter how well or poorly he does. An ESPN poll in 2015 said 34 percent of people think Jordan, who was 52 years of age at the time, could beat a then-30-year-old James in a game of 1-on-1. That's how wonky and clickbait-driven the debate can get. Perhaps one-third of the public might need to be reminded that LeBron continues to bust up Jordan's numbers.

In the third round of the 2014–15 playoffs against the Atlanta Hawks, James eclipsed Jordan's record of 51 games with at least 30 points, 5 rebounds and 5 assists. Kobe, the next closest, had a mere 37 to his name and played in 220 playoff games in his career, as compared to LeBron's 217 games as of 2017. In Game 3 of the 2014–15 Atlanta series, with both Kevin Love and Kyrie Irving injured, James scored 38 points, pulled 18 off the glass and dished out 13 assists for the triple-double, all the while hobbled by injuries to his ankle and back and suffering from cramping. And he started the game 0 for 10 from the field! No player has ever posted a line like that, regular season or postseason. The closest? Charles Barkley back in 1993, who stuck 43 points, 15 boards and 10 dimes in Game 5 of the Western Conference finals. LeBron passed Kareem

Michael Jordan cradles the NBA championship trophy in 1993 following the Chicago Bulls' 99–98 win over the Phoenix Suns for their third straight title.

Abdul-Jabbar and Jerry West for 30-plus-point playoff games (now third all-time) and sits second behind Magic Johnson for most triple-doubles in the postseason, who it should be mentioned, feels more comparable than Jordan ever will be.

Despite all this, LeBron's had to somehow work harder to outlive the legacy of Jordan. It's likely very simple: MJ never lost in the finals, going 6-0. LeBron, just by losing in the NBA Finals, draws the ire of purists. In 2015, James almost equaled Jordan's 1993 record for highest percentage of his team's points, 38.4 percent to 38.3. However, he long ago shattered Jordan's best PER of 32.04 with a mark of 37.39 (2009), which is second all-time to Jordan's draft mate, Hakeem Olajuwon (38.96).

When James launched himself up from the corner in the dying seconds of Game 4 of the 2015 Eastern Conference semifinals versus the Chicago Bulls, it was just the third playoff buzzer beater of his career at that point, which many were quick to point out is in fact the same number Michael Jordan has, and yet His Airness' buzzer beaters are somehow legend. James' first: Game 2 of the 2008–09 Eastern Conference finals against the Orlando Magic. With one second on the clock he drained a shot from three-point land to secure victory. James and the Cavaliers eventually lost that series, but LeBron did just about everything over the course of six games: 38.5 points, 8.3 rebounds, 8.3 assists, 49 percent from the field, all in 44.3 minutes a game. That is some next-level business, but the performance is largely forgotten, as is his PER from that entire playoffs.

Conversely, what isn't soon to fade from memory is Jordan's series-ender versus Cleveland in 1989, a touchstone moment in his career. His finals-finisher a decade later in 1998 was just as great, when in Game 6, he sealed the deal on the Bulls' sixth and last ring with a 20-foot jumper with five seconds left. It wasn't technically a buzzer beater, but considering the circumstances, it was just as big. Plus, what's likely forgotten about that 1998 final is that in the 87–86 Game 6 win, Jordan scored a crucial bucket with a minute to go and then stole the ball from Karl Malone to set up the final points. It would be his last title, and probably the lasting image of a great career despite several comebacks and several retirements.

For James, many may remember the 2014–15 NBA Finals, not for the Golden State Warriors' win, but for the He-Man-like performance of James. It wasn't a one-shot performance for the King; instead it will quite possibly go down as the definition of a one-man team — LeBron versus the Warriors. After losing his fellow star teammates Love and Irving to injury, James lugged Cleveland's bench players on his back as he battled his way game after game. He played 275 minutes out of a possible 298 and averaged 38 points, 13.3 rebounds and 8.8 assists. A horde of voices called for LeBron to be named the MVP despite the series loss. It would have made him the first player to be so named since "Mr. Clutch" Jerry West in 1969. James received four of 11 votes, but it wasn't enough to take the award from the hands of the man who won it — Andre Iguodala, who was picked for his work guarding the Cleveland star. Even with the Warriors' small forward pestering him, James became the first player in the history of the NBA Finals to lead both teams in points, rebounds and assists. That is plain ridiculous.

The following season he avenged his 2015 finals loss, capturing his third title and finally etching himself in lore — not with a clutch shot but with a clutch play now known as "the Block." Running full-speed down the court, he caught up to Iguodala, the man who took his MVP award the year before, and swatted away a potential game-winning basket in the final minutes.

Despite James' three rings to Jordan's six, LeBron's done the work to be called the best ever.

The injured Willis Reed, right, battles with Wilt Chamberlain in Game 7 of the 1970 NBA Finals. Reed's perseverance through injury to help his Knicks win the title was instantly made legend.

OVERCOMING ADVERSITY

Greatness and adversity. Combine the two and you get the stuff of legends. When Isiah Thomas scored 43 points, 25 in one quarter, and added 8 assists and 6 steals in the 1988 NBA Finals while hobbling around on one ankle for the Detroit Pistons, it established a modern-day tale of playing through injury.

The performance was a throwback to what many call the gutsiest comeback in NBA history. That belongs to Willis Reed, the hulking 6-foot-9, 235-pound center of the 1969–70 New York Knicks. It was LA versus New York in a hotly contested NBA championship that came down to the final game. Reed, who had badly injured his right leg in Game 5 after trying to elude the also-ailing Wilt Chamberlain, missed Game 6, and the Lakers forced the pivotal seventh game back in New York at the fabled Madison Square Garden.

Teammates had implored the injured Reed to give them 20 minutes. But as the warm-ups started, Reed was still in the trainer's room.

"I wanted to play," Reed recalled when recounting the story to NBA.com. "That was the championship . . . I didn't want to have to look at myself in the mirror 20 years later and say that I wished I had tried to play."

Reed also remembers that the needle used for the painkillers was huge, and just the act of administering the medicine caused him a lot of pain.

But as he limped to the floor the Garden fans rose up; the players stopped warm-ups, and a tidal wave of appreciative support rained down on Reed and the Knicks.

Dallas Mavericks forward Dirk Nowitzki shoots against the Oklahoma City Thunder during the 2011 Western Conference finals. Nowitzki and Dallas went on to win the NBA title that year.

He didn't throw down many points or hit a buzzer beater. But he was serviceable, keeping Chamberlain to 10 field goals and 2 for 9 in the paint. More telling was the emotional lift it gave his teammates, who ably picked up their center, winning 113–99. It was the Knicks' first-ever title.

Not surprisingly, Michael Jordan added his own power-through-adversity game to the list of the NBA's greatest moments when in 1998 he played in what is known today as "the Flu Game."

The contest is a well-established chronicle — a standout moment from his laundry list of impressive feats.

To recap: It's Game 5 of the NBA Finals and Jordan, who woke up nauseated, dehydrated and fatigued, missed morning practice but donned the jersey come game time. Clearly not himself, Jordan started off slowly but eventually willed himself to drop 30 on the Jazz. With the Bulls victorious, Jordan fell into Scottie Pippen's arms at the end of the game, an enduring image of his exhaustion. They would finish off Utah in Game 6, the sixth and final championship Jordan and the Bulls won. Jordan was named MVP after depositing 39 points to seal the deal. Many thought it was a typical flu, but in 2013, Jordan's former personal trainer would tell the real truth: it was in fact food poisoning the night before the game. A legend was born from a bad pizza ordered late at night in Salt Lake City that did His Airness in. "That was probably the most difficult thing I've ever done," Jordan would say to NBA.com about the night that

became established in NBA lore. It goes down as one of the greatest playoff performances in the history of the NBA.

BUT OVERCOMING ADVERSITY isn't just prevailing when you are physically down and out. It can be stepping up in critical ways when the odds are stacked against you.

On May 13, 2004, not one but two incredible shots occurred back to back in the Western Conference semifinals. After dropping the first two games of the series against the San Antonio Spurs, the LA Lakers stormed back, capped off by their improbable 74–73 Game 5 victory on the road. Derek Fisher's dagger with 0.4 seconds left dispatched the Spurs that evening, and the fact he even got it off with nearly no time remaining was mind-blowing. The fact he actually sunk it established Fisher's rep as a money-ball shooter who rose to the big occasion.

To add to the legend, the unbelievable shot came directly after Tim Duncan hit his own improbable, off-balance 18-footer from the top of the key with Shaquille O'Neal in his face to go ahead by one point. Rare the day it's been when two dying-second shots happen in near synchronicity, and the image of Fisher — running off the court and into the tunnel with a trail of teammates following — is lodged in the collective memory bank of NBA fans.

Dirk Nowitzki, too, had to overcome adversity to earn the respect he rightfully deserved.

Bill Russell loops a hook shot over the head of Jim Krebs of the Los Angeles Lakers in the 1962 NBA Finals. Russell and his Boston Celtics took the series in seven games.

Anyone in the league would let you know that the German is a damn good ball player, but his 48-point performance in the 2011 Western Conference finals versus Oklahoma cemented a long, impressive career. Critics loved to pick apart the mostly hollow theory that the Euro was a choker.

In 2006, the Mavericks made the NBA Finals for the first time in his tenure but lost the championship to the Dwyane Wade–led Miami Heat after leading 2-0. People forget Dirk went off for 50 that year in the Western Conference finals versus Phoenix, scoring 22 in the final frame of Game 5. The following season, the Mavericks lost in the first round to eighth seed Golden State — the same year Nowitzki won MVP — the first time a number one seed lost to an eighth. Despite being the most dominant player in the league, with an NBA Finals trip and an MVP nod, it seemed an asterisk always followed Nowitzki.

Until 2011.

Finally given the chance to expunge his critics, the floppy-haired German hoisted a now underdog Mavs team on his back in Game 1 of the 2011 Western Conference finals against the surging Oklahoma Thunder, who boasted Durant, Westbrook and Harden. Dirk sent a message with 48 points on 12-of-15 shooting, including an astronomical 24 of 24 from the line. He missed just three shots the entire night. Dallas silenced Oklahoma over the course of the series, and Nowitzki exacted revenge on the Heat in a rematch of the 2006 finals, defeating another sparkling trio of James, Wade and Bosh. He finally shed the image of a playoff choker and was named NBA Finals MVP. That 48-point night where he barely missed a basket set the tone, and the rest is history.

BIGS PLAYING BIG

Big moments from physically large men. For years, that was almost exclusively what the NBA offered.

Before the widening of the key and the establishment of the three-point line, bigs ruled the roost — sitting under the bucket in the paint, depositing pick-and-roll plays or scooping up errant outside jumpers for putbacks.

Players like George Mikan, Bill Walton and Kareem Abdul-Jabbar etched legendary postseason performances. Then, in another stratosphere, is Bill Russell.

Most of us probably don't remember the 1962 NBA Finals, but it featured the two storied franchises in the NBA at the time: the Boston Celtics and Los Angeles Lakers. It pitted east versus west and is the last NBA Finals Game 7 to ever go to overtime. Inside the eventual Celtics series win were two monumental performances. Lakers forward Elgin Baylor put up 61 points (and 22 boards) in Game 5 on the road, a finals record that remains today. (Jordan holds the all-time single-game playoff record with 63 points in 1986, the first glimpse into his superstardom.) Baylor's 33 points in one half stood for 25 years until Eric "Sleepy" Floyd broke the record in 1987 (more on that later). In Game 7, though, the tables turned.

Bill Russell dominated the game, putting up 30 points and an astronomical mark of 40 rebounds. Russell collected 370 total

rebounds in 14 playoff games that season — and in his career that is only his third best playoff showing. His averages of 22.9 points, 27 rebounds, and 5.7 assists sealed the deal for the Celtics, who would go on to win several more rings that decade during their dynasty run. Russell finished his playoff career 10-0 in Game 7s, which says a little something about rising to the occasion.

The Lakers also figured in on many great playoff performances, and one was during the 2000 NBA Finals from the man who was as big as they came. Shaq.

At 7-foot-1 and 325 pounds, the Big Aristotle could dominate, but there's a difference between utter dominance and a quiet, controlled supremacy.

When the Lakers beat the Pacers in the 2000 NBA Finals, Shaquille O'Neal posted a not-so-subtle line of 43 points and 19 rebounds in Game 1. It set the tone for a dominant series that saw O'Neal emerge as the go-to man after 21-year-old Kobe Bryant suffered an ankle injury midway through the series when Jalen Rose stepped on said joint. Shaq finished with no fewer than 33 points in any game, and in Game 6, he dropped 41 points and 12 rebounds against a guard-heavy Pacers team that starred Reggie Miller. O'Neal dominated an aging 7-foot-4 Rik Smits in the paint, and with the Pacers hacking Shaq at every opportunity thanks to his poor free-throwing skills, he made enough from the stripe to seal the win.

Hack-a-Shaq has gained in popularity again, most notably in the 2015 second-round playoff series between the Houston Rockets and Los Angeles Clippers. Both big men, DeAndre Jordan and then-center Dwight Howard, are poor free throwers, and both coaches elected to put the other center on the line, which doesn't exactly make for free-flowing basketball. But it can likely be traced back to that 2000 series when Shaq put the Lakers on his shoulders. It was Shaq, not Kobe, who won that series, inspiring future big men and future NBA coaches alike.

Although he may lack the rings of Shaq, Bryant or Jordan, Hakeem Olajuwon took his Houston Rockets to two titles and posted massive playoff numbers during his career that largely go unnoticed.

In 1987, Hakeem the Dream posted a 49-point, 25-rebound, 6-block night, years before he'd win those back-to-back titles in the mid-90s. In 1988, when Houston was swept by the Dallas Mavericks, it wasn't due to a lack of effort from Olajuwon. The Houston big averaged 37.5 points and 16.8 rebounds per game.

And what about those back-to-back titles? The Dream put up averages of 28.9 points and 11 rebounds in 1994, and 33 and 10.3 in 1995.

The 1995 Western Conference finals was the stuff of legend for Olajuwon. Facing off against David Robinson, Dennis Rodman and the San Antonio Spurs, the Houston center dominated, putting up 40-plus points in three of the series' six games, and 39 in the final contest. Robinson cracked 30 only once against Houston, and needing a win in Game 6 to stay alive, he mustered only 19 points.

Olajuwon's record-setting PER was set during the lost playoff opportunity against Dallas in 1987, but he kept on working and was eventually rewarded.

The late great Wilt Chamberlain owns a laundry list of NBA playoff records, including most rebounds in one postseason game (41), despite winning the ultimate prize only twice in his career. The man has his own Wikipedia page just for records he's set. If the argument of greatest playoff performers is based solely on titles, however, Wilt's not even in the conversation.

But there's no doubt he was one of the most dominant postseason performers of his era. He led the NBA in playoff rebounds per game in eight of the 13 seasons his teams made the extra session. And in the five seasons he didn't lead the league, he was second.

Even late in his career, working under the rim for the LA Lakers, Chamberlain was effective. He was able to leave the scoring to others, and at 35 on the 1972 Lakers title winners, he averaged a double-double and led the league in rebounds.

THE GREATEST PLAYOFF PERFORMER YOU'VE NEVER HEARD OF

One man dared take on the mighty LA Lakers in the 1987 playoffs. Before the Bulls made their legendary run in the 90s, there was the Magic Johnson–led Lakers, the crème de la crème of the NBA a decade prior to Jordan's reign. Kareem Abdul-Jabbar and James Worthy rounded out an All-Star cast of characters that would lift the trophy that season, their fourth since 1980. The Golden State Warriors had missed the dance for years but surprisingly sent the Utah Jazz home in the first round after staging an improbable comeback after being down 2-0. They won the clinching Game 5 on the road in Salt Lake City. Their second-round prize? A group of goliaths who had already drunk champagne in 1980, 1982 and 1985. But in 1987, one man dared take on those mighty Lakers. Entering Game 4, Golden State had lost three straight, and by a hefty margin. But that night, the Warriors woke up. Or one man did. His name was Sleepy Floyd.

Eric "Sleepy" Floyd averaged just 12.8 points per game over his admirable 14-year career, but one evening stands above the rest. The 1986–87 season was perhaps his most complete — he made the All-Star Game and averaged 18.8 points and 10.3 assists. But down 3-0 that postseason to the Lakers, Sleepy'd had enough. By the time the game finished, Floyd had single-handedly taken down the best squad of NBA players in the league. At one point, he made 12 field goals in a row. He set NBA records that still stand — 39 points in one half and 29 in the fourth quarter alone. One writer said following the game: "The hair on my neck was standing. The most incredible feeling I've ever had at a sporting event." The YouTube clip of the highlights is equally goosebump-inducing.

The former Georgetown star finished the game with 51 points, etching himself in the basketball history books with an unimaginable, out-of-nowhere performance. The current Warriors team, with the likes of hot-handed Splash Brothers Steph Curry and Klay Thompson, almost feel like heir apparents to Sleepy's record after their first-place finish in the Western Conference in 2014–15 and their march to the 2015 NBA title. Thompson especially: he set the regular-season record for most points in a quarter, dropping an *en fuego* 37 points in the third quarter versus Sacramento midway through the season, finishing 13 of 13 with 9 three-pointers. Perhaps Thompson channeled that epic night of Sleepy Floyd, as now both the regular-season and playoff record for most points in a quarter belong to members of Golden State.

Further, that year Curry set the playoff record for most threes made, and he did it by the second quarter of Game 3 of the Western Conference finals, eclipsing Reggie Miller's mark of 58. Curry and the Warriors still had five wins to go to claim the championship, and in the two quarters and eight games after he set the mark and the

Eric Floyd drives to the basket during the fourth quarter of his record-setting 51-point playoff game against the Los Angeles Lakers in 1987.

Warriors collected their five wins, Curry added 39 more threes. His new mark of 98 seems assailable by only Thompson and himself.

ALTHOUGH CHAMPIONSHIP RINGS may be a starting and end point for some fans, what should make the most difference is how a player affected the outcome of a game or a series. Not one player can do it all and will a team to a championship — the Charles Barkleys and Reggie Millers of the world will always walk around with naked fingers and broken dreams. LeBron couldn't haul a 2007 Cleveland team on his back, and try as he might in 2015, he couldn't do it then, either. (Although he avenged the 2015 loss the next season, he still needed Kyrie Irving's last-minute heroics to get there.) With half his career now in the rearview mirror, LeBron's a perfect example of someone with a brilliant yet flawed NBA Finals record of 3-5. He's won, he's lost, and he's dominated at every step of the way. No one should doubt the man's ability to rise to the occasion. There are many different ways to measure success. Character and heart sometimes don't line up with numbers. On other nights, whether Michael's battling the flu or Isiah's fighting a twisted ankle, greatness occurs and enters into the lore of playoff basketball forever.

UNSUNG HEROES

HASSAN WHITESIDE

ISAIAH THOMAS

MEMPHIS GRIZZLIES

POSITION CENTER / **SHOOTS** RIGHT / **HEIGHT** 7'1" / **WEIGHT** 255 LB. / **DRAFTED** 2007, LOS ANGELES LAKERS, 48TH OVERALL

MARC GASOL 33

MARC GASOL WAS always good — but he was also the younger brother of star NBA player Pau, he of two championship rings with the Los Angeles Lakers. It's taken several years to establish himself among the NBA's elite, but the younger Gasol is finally making his own mark, and the Memphis Grizzlies have become a perennial playoff team in the Western Conference thanks to one of the most dominant centers in the game.

Gasol's early life was spent in Spain, but by the time Pau had been drafted by Memphis, the Gasols had moved to Germantown, Tennessee. Marc played his final two years of high school ball in the Memphis area before returning to his home country to further his craft in the Liga ACB while Pau plied his trade in the NBA. That time in Spain paid off in spades — Marc was named Spanish League MVP in 2008 — and the Lakers drafted the center late in the second round in 2007. His rights were traded later that year — for his brother Pau, in fact, who played seven years in Memphis — and Marc has since become the cornerstone of the Grizzlies. At times, they challenged for best NBA team in 2014–15. Over the following two seasons, with the same core three of Gasol, Zach Randolph and Mike Conley, the Grizz threw opponents around the league into fits, playing old-school, slow-tempo, defense-first basketball that bucked the current trend toward three-point shooting and transition basketball. Much of that

success fell on the shoulders of the 7-foot-1 Gasol, whose emergence as one of the most consistent centers in the game hasn't gone unnoticed.

Marc's always had some serious shoes to fill — his brother was Rookie of the Year and alongside Kobe Bryant dominated the league, winning two championships. And

Marc's weight was always an issue. Not so in 2014–15 — his teammate Mike Conley, upon seeing Gasol compete in the FIBA championship in the summer of 2014, barely recognized his center. "It look[ed] like he lost 50 pounds," Conley remarked early in the season about the former Defensive Player of the Year in 2012–13.

134

That season, he hauled down 7.8 rebounds and had 1.7 blocks playing center for the league's best defensive team, while setting career highs in free-throw percentage at .848 and leading all centers in assists with 318. He'd become an integral part of the Grizzlies, and when he was sidelined the following season for 23 games with a knee injury, the team suffered without him in the lineup.

What he needed to add to his game was offense. The weight loss entering the 2014–15 season immediately made him a scoring threat from beyond the paint, and the combo of deft touch from the 20-foot range with a body big enough to bang inside is lethal. It's also allowed him to hang longer in tough physical games. "You don't have to take the co-pilot seat and let somebody else take over," Gasol said in November. Case in point: his 26-point, 7-rebound and 9-assist performance against fellow big LaMarcus Aldridge and the Portland Trail Blazers at the start of the year, or his 30 points, 6 boards and 6 assists versus the Dirk Nowitzki–led Dallas Mavericks the following week. Marc joined Pau as a 2015 All-Star starter, making them the first siblings to achieve the feat in NBA history.

But it's the intangibles he provides on the court that have truly helped Memphis excel. Whether he's dropping turnaround jumpers or boxing out other big men on the defensive end, Gasol's game has flourished in all facets. In 2015 the Grizz admirably lost in the second round to the eventual champion Golden State Warriors, but it wasn't due to lack of effort on Gasol's part — he averaged 20 and 10 over 11 playoff games. Despite an injury that sidelined him for the second half of the 2015–16 season, Gasol registered his first career triple-double versus the Houston Rockets, the first player on the Grizzlies to accomplish the feat since Pau in 2007.

Trimmer and faster than ever before, Gasol is undeniably one of the best two-way centers in the game today, dropping a career-best 42 points against the Toronto Raptors in January 2017. Edging into his prime NBA years thanks to several seasons in Europe, the man in the middle will be seeking his own ring to wear alongside his brother's hardware. He certainly made a case in 2016–17, averaging career highs in points (19.5) and assists (4.6) and adding a deadly and effective three-point shot to his arsenal.

Marc has finally supplanted his brother as the most effective international center and now ranks among the league's best, period.

CAREER HIGHLIGHTS

- Named NBA Defensive Player of the Year for 2012–13
- Has played in three All-Star Games (2012, 2015, 2017)
- Was an All-NBA First Team selection for 2014–15
- Ranks second in all-time games and minutes played for the Memphis Grizzlies
- Won an Olympic silver medal with the Spanish men's basketball team in Beijing in 2008 and London in 2012

POSITION POWER FORWARD / **SHOOTS** RIGHT / **HEIGHT** 6'7" / **WEIGHT** 230 LB. / **DRAFTED** 2012, GOLDEN STATE WARRIORS, 35TH OVERALL

DRAYMOND GREEN 23

DRAYMOND GREEN MUST have been a circus performer in a former life, because he's been walking a tightrope ever since he entered the NBA, shifting between All-Star and agitator. The 27-year-old has emerged as one of the most unique NBA forwards in recent history — blending size, scoring touch, defensive toughness and a willingness to mix it up with anyone who comes his way. Put simply, there's nobody quite like him.

At 6-foot-7 and 230 pounds, Green's capable of playing both power forward and center, and despite being undersized, he rises to the glass with the ferocity of a bulldog. He's the sparkplug and emotional leader of his team, something the former Michigan State star has been since high school — someone capable of firing himself up and leading his teammates to success. He's already been issued one NBA Finals ring with Golden State. However, this same passion has landed Green in hot water. In 2016 he was dealt an emotional blow when the Warriors blew a 3-1 series lead against Cleveland, and he became Public Enemy Number One to Cavs fans. Some believe it was Green's one-game suspension for kicking LeBron James in Game 4 that sparked the Cavs to victory. "I only know how to be Draymond. That's who I've been my entire life, that's who I'll continue to be," he told the media in December 2016 following a Christmas battle for the ages that rematched the top two teams and witnessed Green get tagged

CAREER HIGHLIGHTS

- Named NBA Defensive Player of the Year for 2016–17
- Named to NBA All-Defensive First Team three times (2014–15, 2015–16, 2016–17)
- Was an All-NBA Second Team selection for 2015–16
- Has played in two All-Star Games (2016, 2017)
- Led the league in steals per game (2.03) in 2016–17

for another technical. His teammates and coaching staff can live with the trash-talking, though — what he brings is the most intangible of intangibles: a motor that doesn't stop firing and a mouth that won't quit. Golden State is fairly confident the shooting prowess of Kevin Durant, Steph Curry and Klay Thompson can compensate for Green's antics if he gets tossed from another playoff game.

It wasn't an easy road to get to the NBA. In high school, Green was a self-appointed class clown and never studied. He even admitted to cheating during a test and missed attending an important basketball camp because his mother wouldn't let him

go until his grades shot up. They did. He led his high school team to two state titles in Michigan and earned a scholarship to Michigan State, close to his hometown of Saginaw. He stayed all four years at Michigan State, making it to the Final Four twice, playing in the final in 2009 during his freshman year and winning the Big Ten championship during his senior year. He was drafted 35th overall in 2012 in what now looks like highway robbery.

Teams weren't sure how to scout him; he was too short to be a power forward — it was suggested by Alvin Gentry, one of Green's coaches, that he's closer to 6'5" — and not fast enough to slide over to small forward. Not being picked until the second round only stoked the burning fire inside one of the NBA's biggest personalities — a classic case of an underdog trying to prove everybody wrong.

Finishing his fifth NBA season, Green has put a unique stamp on the league. In 2015–16, he averaged 14 points per game, 9.5 boards and 7.4 assists, flashy numbers for someone who shifts positions so often. He was also a deadly shot from behind the arc that season, going 39 percent with his 238

three-point attempts. All were career highs.

Green put up lofty numbers in 2016–17, leading the league in steals and cracking the top 10 in assists. He was named an All-Star once again, even though his offensive numbers have dipped since the addition of Durant to the Warriors. (All the Warriors stars saw a dip in numbers, actually.) But the craziest stat of the year for Green is that he posted a triple-double while scoring only four points (the lowest point total ever for a trip-dub), and he was the first since 1986 to record a triple-double that included steals. He had 10 assists, 12 rebounds and 10 steals — his steals nearly tying the NBA record of 11 steals in one game.

Here's an even crazier thing. If the Warriors are going to become the league's next dynasty, it might not be two-time MVP Steph Curry leading the way. Or the lethal three-point shooter Klay Thompson. Or even Kevin Durant, the former MVP and one of the world's best players. It might just be the unsung hero up front, the one who shifts to the middle, slides to the three, sets a pick for his guards and hustles back on defense to steal the rock. It might just be Draymond Green.

POSITION CENTER / **SHOOTS** RIGHT / **HEIGHT** 6'11" / **WEIGHT** 265 LB. / **DRAFTED** 2004, ORLANDO MAGIC, 1ST OVERALL

DWIGHT HOWARD 12

DWIGHT HOWARD MIGHT be a polarizing personality, but his talent is unmistakable. And although he plays the game differently than most, he is an NBA star whose tenure has been impressive in more ways than one.

With a wingspan that stretches across the paint, Howard opted to skip college and try his chances in the pros as a 6-foot-11 18-year-old out of high school, one of the last high schoolers to join the NBA. His physicality was so promising that he was the third high schooler (after Kwame Brown, 2001, and LeBron James, 2003) to be selected first overall when the Orlando Magic picked him in 2004. He made an immediate impression during his rookie season, averaging 12 points and 10 boards and starting all 82 games for the Magic.

Howard quickly turned into an A-plus guy on the back end, causing havoc for opposing players with his length, arm span and efficiency off the glass. Currently ranked 13th all-time in rebounds per game behind Dennis Rodman and ahead of Kareem Abdul-Jabbar, he has led the NBA five times during his career. He was named Defensive Player of the Year for three consecutive seasons starting in 2008–09 and five times has been named to the All-NBA First Team.

When he donned a Superman T-shirt and cape at the 2008 All-Star Game, it showed the goofy, playful side of one of the NBA's elite big men, and he won the Slam Dunk Contest because of his inventiveness. Although it may have endeared him to the fans, his rep on the court remained in sharp contrast, often cited as a respect issue among players.

The perceived rift between him and Kobe Bryant largely overshadowed his year with the LA Lakers in 2012–13 (a team that traded for him to help bring a championship back to Los Angeles). And while Kevin Durant was injured at the beginning of the 2014–15 season, the usually docile Oklahoma Thunder star got up off the bench to bark at Howard. Former player-turned-analyst and legendary trash-talker

Gary Payton said in 2014 that Howard "gets on people's nerves."

This is the same center, mind you, who took the Magic to the NBA Finals in 2009. Howard's run saw the Magic defeat the defending champion Boston Celtics, led up front by Howard's idol, Kevin Garnett. He and the Magic then quickly disposed of LeBron James and the first-place Cleveland Cavaliers. Say what you will about his temperament, he got it done — and yet largely he's been criticized for a personality that doesn't mesh with other players.

He joined James Harden and the Houston Rockets in 2013–14 in their bid to take over the Western Conference from top dogs San Antonio and Golden State. It was a fresh start for the mercurial center with the effusive smile. Too often thrust into the spotlight for reasons unrelated to his on-court performance, Howard proved in Houston that he can share the spotlight with another superstar. In his first of three seasons with the Rockets, Howard put up 18.3 points and 12.2 rebounds per game, but his numbers, as well as his relationship with Harden, declined over time. Once again, some debated whether Howard was a chemistry killer. One thing about Howard that's not up for debate, though, is his terrible free-throw shooting. The 265-pound center hasn't cracked 60 percent from the charity stripe in any season since his rookie year. But he makes up for it in minutes played, gobbling up 35-plus a night his entire career. He missed only 52 games over his first 10 seasons, which highlights his remarkable conditioning.

He was solid in his one season with Atlanta (2016–17), although he can no longer put up point totals like he did as a teenager. He finished with 13.5 points and 12.7 boards. Howard is still one of the top five rebounders in the game, and because of increased diligence to his health — one ESPN story claimed Howard used to scarf down the equivalent of 24 candy bars a day — he is still capable of running the court for 30 minutes per game.

In the 2017 off-season Howard was traded to the Charlotte Hornets for center Miles Plumlee, guard Marco Belinelli and the 41st draft pick.

Maybe he's just the guy people love to hate, a scapegoat in the soap opera behind the scenes in the NBA. No one denies the immense talent on the court and the next-level defense he brings to a team. With a new future in Charlotte alongside the talented Kemba Walker, Howard will silence his critics if he can bring a championship to North Carolina. Maybe that will take the target off the back of one of the league's greatest centers.

CAREER HIGHLIGHTS

- Named an NBA All-Rookie (First Team) in 2004–05
- Named NBA Defensive Player of the Year three times (2009–2011)
- Has played in eight All-Star Games (2007–2014)
- Won the NBA Slam Dunk Contest in 2008
- Is the all-time leading scorer in Orlando

POSITION SMALL FORWARD / **SHOOTS** RIGHT / **HEIGHT** 6'6" / **WEIGHT** 215 LB. / **DRAFTED** 2004, PHILADELPHIA 76ERS, 9TH OVERALL

ANDRE IGUODALA 9

IT'S HARD TO argue the positive impact of a veteran presence on a young team. Sometimes it takes the form of experience on the court, other times, mentorship in the locker room. With Andre Iguodala, his impact shows both on and off the court — a rare combination that's helped turn the Golden State Warriors into a powerhouse and one of the best teams in the NBA.

The 6-foot-6, 215-pound small forward was one of the top draft picks in 2004, selected ninth overall by the Philadelphia 76ers. In Philly, he spent eight seasons in a starting role, averaging 40 minutes a night for several seasons in a row while playing alongside legendary point guard Allen Iverson. Iguodala was indispensable on both sides of the court and had his best scoring season in 2007–08, in which he hit the 20-point mark to go along with 5 boards and 5 helpers every game. But Philadelphia was mired in a funk and never escaped the first round of the playoffs until Iguodala's final season with the club. He played one unmemorable season with Denver before landing on the west coast at the beginning of the Splash Brothers era. As long as Iguodala could accept a role off the bench in the latter half of his career, he had the opportunity to flourish again. He's done more than just flourish: it's been all "Iggy" ever since his arrival in Oakland.

His numbers diminished, of course, but his presence as a defensive stopper against the league's best stars has been

immeasurable — he made the NBA All-Defensive First Team in 2014 — and he's still only in his early 30s. Undoubtedly, his biggest achievement to date is winning the 2015 NBA championship — his first championship ring and Golden State's first in 40 years. Iguodala was named NBA Finals MVP after guarding LeBron James all series, halting the superstar in his tracks. (Although Iguodala would be on the receiving end the following year, when James traveled the length of the court in the final minutes of Game 7 and stuffed Iguodala in what is known as "the Block.")

Raised in Illinois, the small forward played college ball in Arizona, making the Elite Eight his freshman year. (In Arizona, Iguodala was a teammate of future Lakers head coach Luke Walton.) After two successful seasons in college, he finished his final year averaging 12.9 points, 8.4 rebounds and 4.9 assists before heading to the big show. Iguodala's strengths are all across the board. He can shoot, defend,

post up, play big and play small. His all-around game has made him one of the swingmen on the court and a secret weapon off the Warriors bench when either Stephen Curry or Klay Thompson needs a rest. He hits clutch shots, makes clutch stops and always seems to be in the mix. In 2016–17, for example, he dropped 22 points one night versus Memphis, had four steals in a game versus OKC and hauled down 10 boards against Charlotte another night. That's what doing it all means. But most important, he's a calm, veteran voice on a young team — always smiling but uber-competitive when it comes to the court. Iguodala is a big part of the team chemistry in Golden State, that chemistry being one of the main reasons Kevin Durant turned his back on Oklahoma City and joined the Warriors in 2016–17.

A model of consistency throughout his career, Iguodala used to be a glue guy who never got enough respect. Now he's finally getting his due on a high-profile team that

CAREER HIGHLIGHTS

- Named MVP of the NBA Finals in 2015
- Named an NBA All-Rookie (First Team) in 2004–05
- Named to NBA All-Defensive First Team in 2013–14
- Played in the 2012 NBA All-Star Game
- Won an Olympic gold medal with the U.S. men's basketball team in London in 2012

doesn't seem to be slowing down any time soon. If the Warriors continue making the NBA Finals and if Iguodala continues coming off the bench and adding valuable minutes, having one of the most consistent NBA careers of the last generation might be the crafty veteran's legacy. At the very least, he'll go down as one of the most interesting NBA Finals MVPs in the history of the league.

KYLE LOWRY 7

AFTER KYLE LOWRY arrived in Toronto and was thrust into the starting point guard role, the feisty 6-footer set out to prove everyone wrong. He showed the naysayers that he's got all the talent in the world, he can become the heart and soul of a franchise and he is willing to sacrifice everything for the win.

The Philadelphia native was drafted 24th overall in the 2006 draft by the Memphis Grizzlies after just two years at Villanova, where in his final year he tallied 11 points, 3.7 assists and 2.3 steals per game. Villanova, a suburban school in a wealthy part of Philadelphia, appeared to be an odd fit for Lowry. But after being passed over by several high-profile teams like Xavier and North Carolina, the hardscrabble city boy whose father had abandoned him and his brother when he was just 8 years old, stayed close to home and far away all at once. Alvin Williams, former NBA player and coach at Villanova, described Lowry as "a stubborn, hardnosed kid." When his father left, Lowry developed trust issues that permeated his game. But 'Nova needed someone exactly with his skill set: a guard unafraid to drive to the hoop and give them a much-needed edge in the backcourt — things he's still doing in the NBA.

A blown ACL early in his freshman year curtailed his attitude, and Lowry adjusted. By sophomore year, he helped earn a number one seed for Villanova. They lost in the Elite Eight to Florida, and Lowry declared for the NBA. He didn't last long in Memphis, just two seasons, where he was branded a me-first guy, a reputation that's taken years to shake. In February 2009 he was traded to the Houston Rockets.

No one has ever doubted his physical gifts — built like a Mack truck but blessed with the foot speed of a gazelle. He spent his early years splitting time with other point guards in Memphis and Houston, skilled players like Mike Conley Jr., Goran Dragic and Aaron Brooks. It's Lowry's head they questioned, not his heart — what was in between the ears is what coaches wondered about. He also had a problem staying healthy due to his hardnosed style of play, injuring his wrist 10 games into his rookie season and undergoing sports hernia surgery later with Houston, a by-product of his take-no-prisoners, foul-me-if-you-want attitude.

But he began to flourish in Houston, starting 71 games in 2010–11. The two previous seasons he had started exactly zero. Not surprisingly he posted career bests. But after contracting a bacterial infection, he missed time again and was moved to the Toronto Raptors for Gary Forbes and a first-rounder. It wasn't a rosy beginning. The Raps still had Jose Calderon, an established pure point guard. Lowry wasn't pleased with being a backup. So he sulked. A meeting with Raptors general manager Masai Ujiri on the day before training camp transformed the once-stubborn guard into a different man, and he played like it in 2013–14, lifting the Raptors to the playoffs.

The Raptors gutted it out against the Brooklyn Nets that season in the playoffs, taking it to a seventh and final game, with Lowry tasked with the final, game-winning shot. He missed. It stung. But it served notice to the NBA — the Raptors were no joke, and this was Lowry's team, live or die.

After signing a four-year, $48 million deal to stay in Toronto, Lowry owned the role of emotional heartbeat for the franchise during the 2014–15 season, in which he was named a starter in the NBA All-Star Game. Among point guards, he spent

time hanging with the leaders in assist-to-turnover ratio and consistently changed the outcomes of games with his defensive tenacity and timely steals. "It's just the DNA of Kyle," coach Dwane Casey said of his defensive prowess.

The following season he led the Raps deep into the playoffs, although the team finally succumbed to the Cleveland Cavaliers in the conference finals. In 2016–17, Lowry continued soaring upward — his average point total increased to 22.4, his three-point shooting surpassed 40 percent and he was named an All-Star once again. He was neck and neck with LeBron James for most minutes played in the league before a wrist injury after the All-Star break kept him sidelined until the playoffs, the fourth straight year during Lowry's tenure that the Raptors made the postseason. He ended his run at the championship with

CAREER HIGHLIGHTS

- Has played in three All-Star Games (2015–2017)
- Is a five-time NBA Player of the Week
- Named Eastern Conference Player of the Month for December 2014 and January 2016
- Drafted by the Memphis Grizzlies in the first round (24th overall) in 2006
- Is the Raptors' all-time leader in triple-doubles

a sprained ankle and watched from the sidelines as the Cavaliers swept the Raptors in the second round.

The once-disgruntled point guard finally learned to trust his coaches, his teammates and ultimately himself, signing a three-year, $100 million contract with the Raptors in the 2017 off-season. And it appears everyone, fans included, have trusted him back.

POSITION POWER FORWARD / **SHOOTS** LEFT / **HEIGHT** 6'9" / **WEIGHT** 260 LB. / **DRAFTED** 2001, PORTLAND TRAIL BLAZERS, 19TH OVERALL

ZACH RANDOLPH 50

SOME MEN ARE born to bang the glass, born to sit under the rim and bang big bodies and haul down the rock. It may not be the most glamorous job in the NBA, but ever since the likes of Charles Barkley and Dennis Rodman made rebounding fashionable, we've been graced with men like Zach Randolph.

As a freshman at Marion High School in Indiana, he started for the varsity team — a rarity in the basketball-mad state. As a senior he took the Giants to the state championship. He could have leapt straight from high school to the NBA if it weren't for a rule change that now requires athletes to play a minimum of one year of basketball after high school.

Randolph landed at Michigan State in 2000, where in just 20 minutes per game, he put up 10.8 points and 6.7 rebounds for the Spartans — then he opted for the NBA, and he was drafted 19th overall in 2001 by the Portland Trail Blazers. Randolph spent six seasons out west with the "Jail Blazers," a team that played above the law on and off the court. His name showed up on the police blotter along with many other teammates, but ultimately he was never charged with anything and emerged as a valuable power forward, signing a six-year, $84 million contract in 2004. But the big contract was too much for Portland to swallow, and they traded Randolph in 2007 to the New York Knicks for Steve Francis in order to make room for that year's number one pick, Greg Oden, widely considered the biggest bust of the past decade. "Z-Bo," on the other hand, grabbed a career-high 12.5 boards per game for New York before he was dealt to the LA Clippers in 2008.

Another deal landed Randolph in Memphis in 2009, where he established himself as one of the biggest inside presences in the NBA. He's twice made the All-Star Team, and his work under the rim helped turn the Grizzlies from also-rans to playoff contenders.

For the past few seasons, the Grizz consistently finished in the top three in the Southwest Division. Randolph, for his part, just did what he always does. With his trademark headband and left-handed post moves, the 6-foot-9, 260-pound forward formed a formidable pair up front with center Marc Gasol. Case in point: in early January 2015, with Gasol struggling early from the field versus Phoenix, Randolph scored 27 points and added 17 boards, while Gasol scored the crucial baskets down the stretch in a double OT win. There was more to come from Z-Bo: 17 and 22 versus the Detroit Pistons in November, and in a thrilling triple OT victory versus the reigning-champion San Antonio Spurs, Randolph had a monster 21 points and 21 rebounds. He recorded his first career triple-double in 2015–16, putting 28 points, 11 rebounds and 10 assists on the board in a game versus the LA Clippers.

In 2016–17, seeing reduced minutes and fewer starts as Marc Gasol excelled in the center position, Z-Bo was not nearly as effective on the scoreboard. It was in the intangibles that he proved his value and that hard work pays off. Memphis returned to the playoffs for the seventh straight season, although they fell in the first round to the San Antonio Spurs. As a free agent, in the 2017 off-season Randolph signed a two-year $24 million contract with the Sacramento Kings — a hard pill for Memphis fans to swallow.

It's tough to say what makes the Indiana native effective. He isn't a great leaper, or necessarily that long. He has small hands for a big man. But in the stocky mold of Barkley, he's big, he's bad and he creates angles to the hoop that allow him to seemingly haul down boards at will. He's quite simply a throwback to the old days: a thick, mean dude in the post who gets to the basket one way or another.

It wasn't always easy for Randolph. He grew up poor and spent 30 days in juvenile detention for shoplifting jeans because he had only one pair. He missed his entire junior season of high school for possession of stolen guns. But his talent was unmistakable, and his high school coach said in

2012: "I never had a problem once with Zach. We worked hours and hours on that jab step, pull back and shoot the jumper, that little-left handed hook and all the post moves."

He's not likely going to be a Hall of Famer or an MVP. He's often overlooked in favor of the flashy guards and grade-A centers on his teams. But make no mistake — for a franchise to have a player like Randolph in their frontcourt is a blessing, because players willing to grind under the rim the way Randolph does are hard to come by. And generally, they make the difference between winning and losing.

CAREER HIGHLIGHTS

- Named NBA Most Improved Player for 2003–04
- Has played in two All-Star Games (2010, 2013)
- Was an All-NBA Third Team selection for 2010–11
- Ranks in the top 40 all-time in rebounding
- Is the all-time Grizzlies leader in rebounds and two-point field goals

BOSTON CELTICS

POSITION POINT GUARD / **SHOOTS** LEFT / **HEIGHT** 5'9" / **WEIGHT** 185 LB. / **DRAFTED** 2011, SACRAMENTO KINGS, 60TH OVERALL

ISAIAH THOMAS 4

THERE'S THAT OLD cliché, "playing with a chip on your shoulder." For some NBA players, that's a mantra, especially if you're one of the smallest players in the league and a budding superstar. Isaiah Thomas always knew he had the talent, but coaches and GMs had a hard time ignoring his 5-foot-9, 185-pound frame. Thomas, the Boston Celtics and their fans, however, are having the last laugh.

West coast through and through, Thomas played high school ball in Tacoma, a small city in Washington State, before jumping across the country to attend a prep school. Thomas was so small and so good that he and his dad traveled around Tacoma looking for pickup games with adults. It got him in trouble sometimes. He liked to trash-talk, and Thomas found himself constantly avoiding scuffles with grown men who couldn't believe someone that size had just schooled them. A sixteen-year-old Thomas once dropped 51 points in a legendary high school game in Tacoma during his junior year. From prep school, he returned to the west to play three years of college ball for the Washington Huskies. He's still tight with Seattle natives Jason

Terry of the Milwaukee Bucks, Jamal Crawford of the LA Clippers and Nate Robinson, another undersized player who won the dunk contest three times. "We're laid-back, but we've got a killer instinct," Thomas said, and he credits those three for his becoming an NBA player. They, in kind, have referred to Thomas as a "pit bull," "a running back" and "fearless."

Thomas nearly went undrafted in 2011, being picked 60th overall by the Sacramento Kings. He didn't get the chance at big minutes until his final season with the Kings, and by then the franchise opted to move forward with a pass-first point guard to accommodate then-center DeMarcus Cousins. Thomas, a pure scorer, landed in Phoenix with the Suns and found himself among a trio of point guards competing for playing time. His desert sojourn ended quickly. The next chapter in Boston, however, would be his coming-out party.

In 2015–16, Thomas' first full season with Boston, he finished with 22.2 points and over 6 assists a game, taking control of the offense and proving to Sacramento and Phoenix that they made a big mistake by letting him go.

In 2016–17 he upped his point total by nearly 7 points per game. Boston accordingly has soared to test Cleveland for top spot in the east. Thomas finished with 28.9 points and 5.9 assists per game, and he even increased his free-throw shooting to more than 90 percent to finish second in the

CAREER HIGHLIGHTS

- Named an NBA All-Rookie (Second Team) in 2011–12
- Has played in two All-Star Games (2016, 2017)
- Ranked second in NBA free-throw percentage (.912) in 2016–17
- Ranked third in NBA scoring (28.9) in 2016–17
- Named Eastern Conference Player of the Month for January 2017

NBA behind C.J. McCollum and ahead of former MVP Steph Curry. Highlights of the season included a Herculean 52 points at the end of December against the Miami Heat, as well as a near-NBA-record 29 points in the fourth quarter alone. He followed that 52 with a crisp 29 points and 15 dimes versus the Utah Jazz and

44 points and 7 assists versus Eastern Conference rivals the Toronto Raptors, going toe to toe with fellow point guard Kyle Lowry all game. Fourth quarters are really where Thomas has established himself as a superstar, a player with an innate understanding of "clutch." It's an X factor, that swagger you need to be the best. "The fourth quarter isn't for everyone," he famously said earlier in the season as he began torching teams at crunch time.

"Zeke," as he's known, also gives back to Tacoma, running a charity tournament called Memorial Day Zeke-End. It's a chance for him to reconnect with the community (the gym he grew up playing in is now named after him) and chow down on his favorite food — fish and chips. He also showed true heart in the 2017 playoffs when he suited up for Game 1 despite the tragic passing of his younger sister in a car

accident the day before. The entire NBA lauded his spirit, and he punctuated the moment two weeks later with a heroic 53 points in an overtime win versus the Washington Wizards in the second round.

With his trademark headband (an ode to Terry, who also sports one), it's easy to see the whirling dervish on the court. Thomas slides, glides and drifts through traffic like a character in a video game. The point guard's been a relative bargain at just over $6 million in 2016–17, but that won't last long — when you're in the top three in scoring at 28.9 points per game, the Benjamins start flying, and he's sure to see a contract extension with Boston. "The Little Ticket" couldn't be a better nickname because he's the one driving the box office these days. Thomas has proven that good things come in small packages, but can the NBA's smallest player deliver a championship?

KEMBA WALKER 15

KEMBA HUDLEY WALKER of the Bronx, New York, burst onto the scene suddenly, like a house on fire — a small but tough point guard who could score at will no matter what the level. The undisputed leader of the Charlotte Hornets since he landed in the league, Walker's been pulling the North Carolina basketball franchise like a lead pack dog, and slowly but surely, the Hornets are crawling out of the NBA's basement. Success or failure will fall on the shoulders of Walker, who has proven size doesn't matter when you're all heart.

Walker made a name for himself on the national stage playing in the NCAA Final Four, carrying the UConn Huskies to the championship in 2011 during his junior year. Walker was hotter than a ghost pepper for weeks that spring, dropping 150 points en route to the Big East title, and he continued his hot streak while leading the third-seeded Huskies past Butler in the NCAA final. During the 2011 Big East tourney, UConn put up five wins in five days. (Check out Walker's crossover, step-back winner versus Pittsburgh on YouTube. Seriously.) What followed was an undefeated run to cast Walker into NCAA lore. It's arguably one of the hottest runs a college player's ever put together, and he's carried the legend of 2011 ever since.

Walker was named outstanding player of the tournament and elected to enter the NBA Draft rather than play a final year. He was selected ninth overall by the Michael Jordan–owned Charlotte Hornets (then known as the Bobcats), behind first overall Kyrie Irving and in front of Isaiah Thomas, who was the 60th and final pick of the draft.

What makes Walker so damn good? You could say it's all in the footwork for the point guard. As a youth he possessed not only blinding speed on the court but also coordination that led him to moonlight as a dancer at the famed Apollo Theater. (Hence the crazy amount of space he creates on his patented step-back.) Growing up in New York City, let alone the hard-nosed Bronx, is tough enough. But to be

CAREER HIGHLIGHTS

- Played in the 2017 NBA All-Star Game
- Finished third in minutes played (2,885) in 2015-16
- Is a five-time NBA Player of the Week
- Drafted by the Charlotte Hornets in the first round (9th overall) in 2011
- Named Final Four Most Outstanding Player in 2011

2011–12 season 7-59, the worst winning percentage in NBA history. The freshly drafted Walker took the losses hard after his college successes the year before. "It [was] killing me," he recalled in 2016 when asked about his rookie season.

Walker went to work, fixing his jump shot and three-point angles instead of polishing a predictable dribble-and-drive game. His shooting percentage increased, and things in Charlotte started to improve under a new head coach. The basket-first point guard is atypical in that he's not an assist-first guy, but he has learned to share the ball with his teammates while still driving to the basket like he did in the Bronx. In the past two seasons he's elevated his game to become one of the NBA's must-watch stars, and he now averages nearly 23 points a night. The difference? Bust-out games, like the 40-10-7 stat line he ripped against Toronto early in the 2016–17 season, or the 37 he dropped on the Cavaliers on New Year's Eve.

Walker played in the 2017 All-Star Game. It was the first time he'd been named to the team, and that's always a time for reflection, especially for an underappreciated, undersized guard whom people had always doubted. Throughout 2016–17 he hovered around the 40 percent mark for his three-point shooting, which isn't exceptional, but considering he's in the top 10 for attempts, it's a definite improvement from behind the arc and a weapon he'll continue to employ.

With the addition of several more pieces, such as newly acquired Dwight Howard, Charlotte could be a team to watch in the next couple of years as Walker heads into his prime. Plus, he's signed for $12 million a year through 2019.

Perhaps the coolest thing about Walker is how multitalented he is — singing, rapping and dancing off the court, he's an infectious personality with a big smile. The footwork's always been there, as has the bounce in his step, and just like he did when he was playing on the tough courts of New York, he continues to defy the odds.

the best and rise above you have to play your guts out, everywhere, all the time. And every time, there was Walker, like lightning to the basket. Legend has it he scored 80 points one game without hitting a single three.

In his first three seasons as a full-time starter in Charlotte, Walker — listed generously at 6-foot-1 and 184 pounds — was remarkably consistent, averaging just over 17 points a game. But Charlotte was doing poorly and finished the lockout-shortened

MIAMI HEAT

POSITION CENTER / **SHOOTS** RIGHT / **HEIGHT** 7'0" / **WEIGHT** 265 LB. / **DRAFTED** 2010, SACRAMENTO KINGS, 33RD OVERALL

HASSAN WHITESIDE 21

IT WAS ONCE rare for an NBA player to come out of nowhere, to be a blip on the radar before ascending to star status, but this has become a recurring theme in the current NBA. (Jeremy Lin of "Linsanity" fame and former Bulls star Jimmy Butler both come to mind in recent years.) In a league where only 150 starting jobs are available at any given time, many positions are predetermined. Some, however, are simply taken by the hungriest. So when Hassan Whiteside meekly arrived onto the NBA scene in the second round of the 2010 draft, selected 33rd by the Sacramento Kings, no one could have predicted his rise to being one of the game's premier centers.

Born in Gastonia, North Carolina, the seven-footer wasn't a sure thing. The height was there, but the work ethic and talent would take time to develop. He played high school ball at the relatively unheard of Patterson School before suiting up for the relatively unheard of Marshall University, where he played just one season. In that short time, Whiteside led his team with more than five blocks per game (which was tops among all college players). He declared for the NBA, but in hindsight perhaps he wasn't ready. A former D-League coach stated that bigs take longer to develop, and Whiteside certainly fits that description. But beyond the development of skills, focus and attitude were key issues in Whiteside's slow growth. (Okay, it was mostly attitude.) After being drafted, Whiteside started his NBA career with the Kings' D-League team in Reno, Nevada — a demotion he didn't take lightly. A knee injury derailed the remainder of his season. Looking back on his troubled rookie year, in 2015 Whiteside said, "I always had this cloud over me."

He played just eight minutes over two seasons for the Kings organization and

season with 11.8 points, 10 boards and 2.6 blocks per game.

At the beginning of 2015–16, he signed a four-year-max contract to the tune of $98 million. Whiteside penned these words on The Players' Tribune: "I've played on eight teams since college — from Reno to Sioux Falls to Sichuan, China. I am not ready for there to be a ninth." (This number is likely even higher; he also played in the basketball mecca of Lebanon.) Miami gave the journeyman a home for the first time as a new era was dawning. James and Wade had left for greener pastures, and Chris Bosh remained sidelined with ongoing blood-clot issues.

The keys to Whiteside's success are abnormally long arms and freakish athleticism in the post, where he can play equally well facing the basket as he can with his back to the rim. But it's on the other side of the ball that he dominates the basketball ecosystem and truly thrives. He has become one of the best shot-blockers in the game, a rim protector of the highest quality, posting numbers that should make other centers blush. In 2015–16, he put up 14 points a game, hauled down an average of 12 boards and swatted 3.7 shots away, leading the league in blocks. In 2016 versus Denver, Whiteside posted an unreal stat line: 19 points, 17 rebounds and 11 blocks. This wasn't even the first time he had a triple-double with blocks, and he's accomplished the feat four times now.

Miami may be rebuilding on the fly, but they still managed to rattle off a midseason winning streak of 13 games in 2016–17 with Whiteside, point guard Goran Dragic and a cast of young, burgeoning forwards. This is after starting the season 11-30. It bodes well for the young team, whose commitment to staying the course with Whiteside in the middle could become a signature for the Miami franchise. All he needed was for someone to believe in him — now, he's got Miami fans believing another playoff run in the near future isn't such a far-fetched dream.

CAREER HIGHLIGHTS

- Named to NBA All-Defensive Second Team in 2015–16
- Led the NBA in blocks per game (3.68) in 2015–16
- Led the NBA in rebounds per game (14.1) in 2016–17
- D-League champion in 2012–13
- NCAA Division I blocks leader in 2010

bounced around the D-League and international teams before arriving in South Beach. The change was career altering, and being part of a crew headed by famous coach and manager Pat Riley and surrounded by superstar, championship-winning veterans such as LeBron James, Dwyane Wade and Chris Bosh provided the magic elixir the center needed to succeed. He finished his breakout 2014–15

NBA REGULAR-SEASON MVP WINNERS

2016–17: Russell Westbrook, Oklahoma City Thunder

2015–16: Stephen Curry, Golden State Warriors

2014-15: Stephen Curry, Golden State Warriors

2013-14: Kevin Durant, Oklahoma City Thunder

2012-13: LeBron James, Miami Heat

2011-12: LeBron James, Miami Heat

2010-11: Derrick Rose, Chicago Bulls

2009-10: LeBron James, Cleveland Cavaliers

2008-09: LeBron James, Cleveland Cavaliers

2007-08: Kobe Bryant, Los Angeles Lakers

2006-07: Dirk Nowitzki, Dallas Mavericks

2005-06: Steve Nash, Phoenix Suns

2004-05: Steve Nash, Phoenix Suns

2003-04: Kevin Garnett, Minnesota Timberwolves

2002-03: Tim Duncan, San Antonio Spurs

2001-02: Tim Duncan, San Antonio Spurs

2000-01: Allen Iverson, Philadelphia 76ers

1999-00: Shaquille O'Neal, Los Angeles Lakers

1998-99: Karl Malone, Utah Jazz

1997-98: Michael Jordan, Chicago Bulls

1996-97: Karl Malone, Utah Jazz

1995-96: Michael Jordan, Chicago Bulls

1994-95: David Robinson, San Antonio Spurs

1993-94: Hakeem Olajuwon, Houston Rockets

1992-93: Charles Barkley, Phoenix Suns

1991-92: Michael Jordan, Chicago Bulls

1990-91: Michael Jordan, Chicago Bulls

1989-90: Earvin Johnson, Los Angeles Lakers

1988-89: Earvin Johnson, Los Angeles Lakers

1987-88: Michael Jordan, Chicago Bulls

1986-87: Earvin Johnson, Los Angeles Lakers

1985-86: Larry Bird, Boston Celtics

1984-85: Larry Bird, Boston Celtics

1983-84: Larry Bird, Boston Celtics

1982-83: Moses Malone, Philadelphia 76ers

1981-82: Moses Malone, Houston Rockets

1980-81: Julius Erving, Philadelphia 76ers

1979-80: Kareem Abdul-Jabbar, Los Angeles Lakers

1978-79: Moses Malone, Houston Rockets

1977-78: Bill Walton, Portland Trail Blazers

1976-77: Kareem Abdul-Jabbar, Los Angeles Lakers

1975-76: Kareem Abdul-Jabbar, Los Angeles Lakers

1974-75: Bob McAdoo, Buffalo Braves

1973-74: Kareem Abdul-Jabbar, Milwaukee Bucks

1972-73: Dave Cowens, Boston Celtics

1971-72: Kareem Abdul-Jabbar, Milwaukee Bucks

1970-71: Kareem Abdul-Jabbar, Milwaukee Bucks

1969-70: Willis Reed, New York Knicks

1968-69: Wes Unseld, Baltimore Bullets

1967-68: Wilt Chamberlain, Philadelphia 76ers

1966-67: Wilt Chamberlain, Philadelphia 76ers

1965-66: Wilt Chamberlain, Philadelphia 76ers

1964-65: Bill Russell, Boston Celtics

1963-64: Oscar Robertson, Cincinnati Royals

1962-63: Bill Russell, Boston Celtics

1961-62: Bill Russell, Boston Celtics

1960-61: Bill Russell, Boston Celtics

1959-60: Wilt Chamberlain, Philadelphia Warriors

1958-59: Bob Pettit, St. Louis Hawks

1957-58: Bill Russell, Boston Celtics

1956-57: Bob Cousy, Boston Celtics

1955-56: Bob Pettit, St. Louis Hawks

Six-time regular-season MVP Kareem Abdul-Jabbar of the Los Angeles Lakers scores two points in the 1980 Western Conference semifinals against the Phoenix Suns.

NBA ALL-STAR GAME MVP WINNERS

2016–17: Anthony Davis, New Orleans Pelicans

2015–16: Russell Westbrook, Oklahoma City Thunder

2014-15: Russell Westbrook, Oklahoma City Thunder

2013-14: Kyrie Irving, Cleveland Cavaliers

2012-13: Chris Paul, Los Angeles Clippers

2011-12: Kevin Durant, Oklahoma City Thunder

2010-11: Kobe Bryant, Los Angeles Lakers

2009-10: Dwyane Wade, Miami Heat

2008-09: Shaquille O'Neal, Phoenix Suns (Tie)

2008-09: Kobe Bryant, Los Angeles Lakers (Tie)

2007-08: LeBron James, Cleveland Cavaliers

2006-07: Kobe Bryant, Los Angeles Lakers

2005-06: LeBron James, Cleveland Cavaliers

2004-05: Allen Iverson, Philadelphia 76ers

2003-04: Shaquille O'Neal, Los Angeles Lakers

2002-03: Kevin Garnett, Minnesota Timberwolves

2001-02: Kobe Bryant, Los Angeles Lakers

2000-01: Allen Iverson, Philadelphia 76ers

1999-00: Shaquille O'Neal, Los Angeles Lakers (Tie)

1999-00: Tim Duncan, San Antonio Spurs (Tie)

1997-98: Michael Jordan, Chicago Bulls

1996-97: Glen Rice, Charlotte Hornets

1995-96: Michael Jordan, Chicago Bulls

1994-95: Mitch Richmond, Sacramento Kings

1993-94: Scottie Pippen, Chicago Bulls

1992-93: John Stockton, Utah Jazz (Tie)

1992-93: Karl Malone, Utah Jazz (Tie)

1991-92: Earvin Johnson, Los Angeles Lakers

1990-91: Charles Barkley, Philadelphia 76ers

1989-90: Earvin Johnson, Los Angeles Lakers

1988-89: Karl Malone, Utah Jazz

1987-88: Michael Jordan, Chicago Bulls

1986-87: Tom Chambers, Seattle SuperSonics

1985-86: Isiah Thomas, Detroit Pistons

1984-85: Ralph Sampson, Houston Rockets

1983-84: Isiah Thomas, Detroit Pistons

1982-83: Julius Erving, Philadelphia 76ers

1981-82: Larry Bird, Boston Celtics

1980-81: Nate Archibald, Boston Celtics

1979-80: George Gervin, San Antonio Spurs

1978-79: David Thompson, Denver Nuggets

1977-78: Randy Smith, Buffalo Braves

1976-77: Julius Erving, Philadelphia 76ers

1975-76: Dave Bing, Washington Bullets

1974-75: Walt Frazier, New York Knicks

1973-74: Bob Lanier, Detroit Pistons

1972-73: Dave Cowens, Boston Celtics

1971-72: Jerry West, Los Angeles Lakers

1970-71: Lenny Wilkens, Seattle SuperSonics

1969-70: Willis Reed, New York Knicks

1968-69: Oscar Robertson, Cincinnati Royals

1967-68: Hal Greer, Philadelphia 76ers

1966-67: Rick Barry, San Francisco Warriors

1965-66: Adrian Smith, Cincinnati Royals

1964-65: Jerry Lucas, Cincinnati Royals

1963-64: Oscar Robertson, Cincinnati Royals

1962-63: Bill Russell, Boston Celtics

1961-62: Bob Pettit, St. Louis Hawks

1960-61: Oscar Robertson, Cincinnati Royals

1959-60: Wilt Chamberlain, Philadelphia Warriors

1958-59: Bob Pettit,
St. Louis Hawks (Tie)

1958-59: Elgin Baylor,
Minneapolis Lakers (Tie)

1957-58: Bob Pettit,
St. Louis Hawks

1956-57: Bob Cousy,
Boston Celtics

1955-56: Bob Pettit,
St. Louis Hawks

1954-55: Bill Sharman,
Boston Celtics

1953-54: Bob Cousy,
Boston Celtics

1952-53: George Mikan,
Minneapolis Lakers

1951-52: Paul Arizin,
Philadelphia Warriors

1950-51: Ed Macauley,
Boston Celtics

Three-time All-Star Game
MVP Michael Jordan of the
Chicago Bulls slam dunks
the ball.

NBA FINALS MVP WINNERS

2016–17: Kevin Durant, Golden State Warriors

2015–16: LeBron James, Cleveland Cavaliers

2014-15: Andre Iguodala, Golden State Warriors

2013-14: Kawhi Leonard, San Antonio Spurs

2012-13: LeBron James, Miami Heat

2011-12: LeBron James, Miami Heat

2010-11: Dirk Nowitzki, Dallas Mavericks

2009-10: Kobe Bryant, Los Angeles Lakers

2008-09: Kobe Bryant, Los Angeles Lakers

2007-08: Paul Pierce, Boston Celtics

2006-07: Tony Parker, San Antonio Spurs

2005-06: Dwyane Wade, Miami Heat

2004-05: Tim Duncan, San Antonio Spurs

2003-04: Chauncey Billups, Detroit Pistons

2002-03: Tim Duncan, San Antonio Spurs

2001-02: Shaquille O'Neal, Los Angeles Lakers

2000-01: Shaquille O'Neal, Los Angeles Lakers

1999-00: Shaquille O'Neal, Los Angeles Lakers

1998-99: Tim Duncan, San Antonio Spurs

1997-98: Michael Jordan, Chicago Bulls

1996-97: Michael Jordan, Chicago Bulls

1995-96: Michael Jordan, Chicago Bulls

1994-95: Hakeem Olajuwon, Houston Rockets

1993-94: Hakeem Olajuwon, Houston Rockets

1992-93: Michael Jordan, Chicago Bulls

1991-92: Michael Jordan, Chicago Bulls

1990-91: Michael Jordan, Chicago Bulls

1989-90: Isiah Thomas, Detroit Pistons

1988-89: Joe Dumars, Detriot Pistons

1987-88: James Worthy, Los Angeles Lakers

1986-87: Earvin Johnson, Los Angeles Lakers

1985-86: Larry Bird, Boston Celtics

1984-85: Kareem Abdul-Jabbar, Los Angeles Lakers

1983-84: Larry Bird, Boston Celtics

1982-83: Moses Malone, Philadelphia 76ers

1981-82: Earvin Johnson, Los Angeles Lakers

1980-81: Cedric Maxwell, Boston Celtics

1979-80: Earvin Johnson, Los Angeles Lakers

1978-79: Dennis Johnson, Seattle SuperSonics

1977-78: Wes Unseld, Washington Bullets

1976-77: Bill Walton, Portland Trail Blazers

1975-76: Jo Jo White, Boston Celtics

1974-75: Rick Barry, Golden State Warriors

1973-74: John Havlicek, Boston Celtics

1972-73: Willis Reed, New York Knicks

1971-72: Wilt Chamberlain, Los Angeles Lakers

1970-71: Kareem Abdul-Jabbar, Milwaukee Bucks

1969-70: Willis Reed, New York Knicks

1968-69: Jerry West, Los Angeles Lakers

Three-time finals MVP Tim Duncan of the San Antonio Spurs drives to the basket past the Charlotte Hornets defense.

ACKNOWLEDGMENTS

FIRST, I'D LIKE to thank my editors, Steve Cameron and Julie Takasaki, whose sharp eyes for detail and ability to come up with multiple ways of saying rebounds and assists are exceptional qualities. Their patience, guidance and steady hands are all over this book. I'd like to express my gratitude to publisher Lionel Koffler and all the staff at Firefly Books, as well as copyeditor Patricia MacDonald and designer Matt Filion, for their help in molding and shaping *Basketball Now!* — books are very much a collaboration, and the hard work of everyone involved is much appreciated.

Personally, I'd like to thank my parents, David and Esther-Jo, and my sister, Michelle, whose support has always been unwavering. While many friends and former colleagues have inspired me while writing this book, I'd like to particularly thank Jonathan and Andy, who watched a multitude of games with me over the past several seasons, especially our hometown Raptors, and who smiled patiently as I babbled on about my man crush for Steph Curry or the Raptors' inability to defend the pick and roll. I'd like to give a special shout-out to two of my oldest friends, Josh and Micah, for all those games of horse and twenty-one in my alleyway when we were kids growing up in Vancouver (RIP Grizzlies). Like for many kids, those moments formed the nucleus of my earliest basketball memories (beyond the Bulls' first three-peat and the Grizzlies' franchise-changing drafting of Bryant "Big Country" Reeves). I can think of nothing better than spending a lazy summer afternoon shooting hoops in the sun, and it was during those formative years that I learned what it means to love sport, friends and lazy days on the courts. Finally, I'd like to thank you, the basketball fan, for reading!

– Adam Elliott Segal

Steph Curry faces off against LeBron James in Game 1 of the 2017 NBA Finals.

PROFILE INDEX

PHOTO CREDITS

ICON SPORTSWIRE

Aaron Lavinsky/Zuma Press 76, 123
Armando L. Sanchez/Zuma Press 113
Carlos Gonzalez/Zuma Press 104, 120, 121,
Charles King/Zuma Press 85, 95
Charles Trainor Jr./Zuma Press 79, 86, 150, 151
Chris Sweda/Zuma Press 28, 77
Curtis Compton/Zuma Press 89, 138, 139, 141, 142
Dan Honda/Zuma Press 135
David Santiago/Zuma Press 29, 30, 51
David T. Foster/Zuma Press 156
Ed Crisostomo/Zuma Press 27, 54
Hector Acevedo/Zuma Press 46, 108, 109, 145
Hector Amezcua/Zuma Press 119
Icon Sportswire 64, 65, 93, 103, 107
Jeff Siner/Zuma Press 18, 136, 148, 149
Jim Cowsert/Zuma Press 74
Jose Carlos Fajardo/Zuma Press 14
Kevin Reece 155
Kevin Sullivan/Zuma Press 102
Kirthmon F. Dozier/Zuma Press 17
Kyusung Gong/Zuma Press 55, 146
Leah Klafczynski/Zuma Press 12, 23, 40, 50, 52, 57, 87
Mike Cardew/Zuma Press 22
Nhat V. Meyer/Zuma Press 58, 158
Nuccio Dinuzzo/Zuma Press 45, 53
Patrick Farrell/Zuma Press 78
Phil Masturzo/Zuma Press 61
Prensa Internacional/Zuma Press 124
Ray Chavez/Zuma Press 2, 62
Ricardo Ramirez Buxeda/Zuma Press 118
Stephen Lew 13, 91, 92
Stephen M. Dowell/Zuma Press 9, 15, 63, 94, 140
Steve Nurenberg/Zuma Press 24, 43, 88, 117
Steven M. Falk/Zuma Press 116
Terrence Antonio James/Zuma Press 5, 44
Torrey Purvey 6, 10, 16, 21, 31, 56, 59, 106, 110, 112, 122, 134
Troy Taormina/Action Images/Panoramic 20
Winslow Townson/Action Images/Panoramic 132, 147

Front Cover:
Aaron Lavinsky/Zuma Press (Wiggins)
Mark Alberti (James)
Stephen Lew (Davis)
Stephen M. Dowell/Zuma Press (Curry)
Torrey Purvey (DeRozan, Westbrook)

Back Cover:
Carlos Gonzalez/Zuma Press (Towns)
Jim Cowsert/Zuma Press (Lillard, Nowitzki)

AP PHOTO

Andy Clayton-King 111
AP Photo 34, 153
Bill Kostroun 99
Bob Leverone 48
Darren Abate 26
Diane Bondareff 37
Elise Amendola 39
Eric Christian Smith 80
Eric Gay 19, 25, 81, 83, 90
Eric Risberg 131
George Widman 36
Gerald Herbert 49, 101
Greg Wahl-Stephens 96, 98
Harold P. Matosian 129
Jeff Chiu 42, 82
Marcio Jose Sanchez 137
Marty Lederhandler 32
Matt York 47
Mike Stone 128
Morry Gash 143
Peter Southwick 100
Scott Troyanos 126
Steven Senne 84
Susan Sterner 35
Tim Johnson 130
Tony Dejak 60
Tony Gutierrez 114, 115, 144

GETTY IMAGES

Bettmann/Contributor 127
Carl Iwasaki 69
Jesse D. Garrabrant 73
Nathaniel S. Butler 67, 68
NBA Photos/Bill Smith 71
Walter Iooss Jr. 70

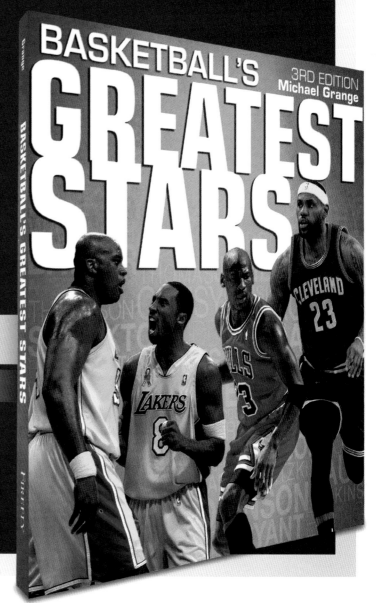